GERMAN VOCABULARY TOOLKIT

Published by Collins Educational
An imprint of HarperCollins*Publishers* Ltd
77–85 Fulham Palace Road
London
W6 8JB

www.**Collins**Education.com
On-line support for schools and colleges

© HarperCollins*Publishers* Ltd 2002
First published 2002

ISBN 0-00-713582 3

British Library Cataloguing in Publication Data
A catalogue record for this book is available from the British Library.

Publishing manager Anna Samuels
Edited by Antonia Maxwell
Design and illustration by Pumpkin House
Cover design by Blue Pig Design Co
Production by Katie Morris
Printed and bound by Printing Express Ltd., Hong Kong

You might also like to visit
www.**fire**andwater.co.uk
The book lover's website

CONTENTS

Welcome to the German Vocabulary Toolkit!

The aim of this book is to help you to learn the vocabulary which you will need to do well in the GCSE examination in German. The vocabulary listed in the book is based on the word lists in the specifications of the Edexcel awarding body and will be particularly useful if you are preparing for an Edexcel examination.

You will not be allowed to use a dictionary in your examinations, so it is important that you have a good knowledge of vocabulary to back you up. The more words you know, the easier you will find it to do the questions well. Just as you can't build a house without bricks, you can't write in German without the words to put into the sentences.

Structure of the book

This book is arranged to match the vocabulary topics of the specifications common to all the awarding bodies. The titles of these topics are given at the beginning of each section. In addition, each section uses colour to show the gender of the nouns. Masculine nouns ('der') are printed in blue; feminine nouns ('die') are printed in pink; neuter nouns ('das') are printed in orange. Plurals are printed in brown, verbs are printed in dark green, and adjectives are printed in light green. All other types of words are printed in purple. (There is some evidence to show that colour coding helps one remember which gender group a word belongs to by picturing the colour groups on the page.)

For each topic, vocabulary from the Higher Level is marked by an asterisk.

The activities

After the list of words in each topic, there are a number of activities which will help you check whether you have learned the words. You should only do these activities when you have finished learning the vocabulary.

It would be possible to do the activities by writing the answers into the book, but it would be much better to write your answers onto a separate piece of paper. You could then do the activities several times – the more often you use the words the better they will become fixed in your memory. You will also be able to revise as the exam approaches.

Maybe you have bought the book a few weeks before the examination! In this case, do the exercises first. This will help you to find out which words you know and which ones you need to learn.

You will find the answers to the activities at the back of the book. Only look at the answers once you have done the exercises! Then you will find out which words you really have learnt. Don't look first! It won't help you to learn the words; it will only make you think that you know more than you really do.

You may have some answers which are different from the ones provided. This could well be the case. Don't automatically assume that you are wrong. Check with your teacher to see if your answer is also possible. (Maybe you could write to us at Collins and we could include your answers in a future edition!)

Vocabulary learning

Vocabulary learning is an essential part of learning a foreign language and there are no short cuts. You have to build up your vocabulary by learning it slowly and gradually. Good linguists have a large vocabulary.

If you manage to learn ten words every day from Monday to Friday and use the weekend to revise them, you will learn fifty words a week. If you learn 50 words a week, you will learn 200 words in a month. 200 words every month means that you learn 2400 in a year. And 2400 words is more than enough for GCSE!

People learn vocabulary in different ways. You need to find the way which is best for you and use it regularly. In the next section we give you some tips on how to learn vocabulary. Try some of them out and you may find that learning vocabulary is more fun than you thought it was.

Viel Spaß!

Tips on vocabulary learning

1   Keep this book with you all the time. Use it when you have a spare moment. Every little helps! Test yourself regularly. Tick the words you really do know and concentrate on the ones you need to learn.

2   Use this book often: when you are waiting for the bus; on the bus; when you have a few minutes to spare at home.

3   Write out the words which you are finding difficult to learn. Write them slowly and carefully. Write them four or five times each.

4   Keep a separate notebook for words which you come across which are not in this book. Use this notebook in the same way: go through it regularly, so that you learn these words too. The more words you know, the easier you will find it to do the tests in the examination.

5   Make a set of vocabulary cards. Write the English word on one side of the card and the German word on the other. Go through the cards, testing yourself on the words. Put the words you know to one side. If you don't know a word, put it at the bottom of the pack, so that it comes up again until you really do know it.

6   Get your parents, a relation or a friend to test you on the words you have to learn. It doesn't matter if they don't speak German. If they aren't sure if you got the word right, get them to ask you to spell it.

7   Write down the words on little notes and put them around the house in places where you will see them regularly, e.g. by the television; in the bathroom; on the stairs; by the computer; by your bed; on the fridge. Tell your parents this is a vital part of your learning for GCSE!

8   Use your vocabulary cards in the same way. Put one by the front door. Every time you come in or go out, look at the English word, say the foreign word, then turn the card over to see if you got it right. When you are sure you know the word, change the card for another one.

9 Say the words out loud when you are learning them. It helps you to remember them.

10 Make a cassette to help you learn the words. Write down a list of the English words and the German words. Speak the English words out loud one by one onto the cassette. After each English word, say the German word to yourself twice, without speaking out loud. This leaves a gap on the tape. When you have finished, play the tape and try to say the foreign word in the gap on the tape. When you can do this quickly for all the words, you will have learnt them. You can use the tape on your walkman.

11 If you are having difficulties remembering a word, ask a friend (or a teacher) to ask you what it is every time they pass you in the corridor in school. Make it into a kind of joke. You'll soon learn it then!

12 And don't forget to try and learn a small number of words each day. Remember: 10 a day = 50 a week = 200 a month = 2400 a year =

Success at GCSE!

A note to parents

You can help your son or daughter by supporting them in their vocabulary learning. Even if you don't speak German, you can probably tell whether they know the word or not. If you are not sure, ask your son or daughter to spell it.

Allow your child to put some of the vocabulary learning tips into practice. It may mean having a lot of notes around your home and will make dusting difficult for a while - but you will be pleased when your child passes GCSE!

Take an interest in their vocabulary-learning and encourage them to do it. Try to have a regular time each day (e.g. after a meal) when you listen to the words they have learnt. Most children need a structure to help them learn. You can provide that.

der Bart	beard
der Bruder	brother
der Erwachsene	grown-up
der Familienname	surname
der Freund	friend
der Geburtstag	birthday
der Großvater	grandfather
der Hahn	cockerel
der Hamster	hamster
der Herr	gentleman
der Huhn	hen
der Hund	dog
der Junge	boy
der Körper	body
der Mann	man
der Nachbar	neighbour
der Name	name
der Onkel	uncle
der Opa/Opi	granddad
der Papagei	parrot
der Schwager	brother-in-law
der Sohn	son
der Stiefvater	stepfather*
der Vater	father
Vati	daddy
der Verwandte	relative
der Vetter	cousin (male)
der Vogel	bird
der Vorname	first name
der Wellensittich	budgerigar
der Zwilling	twin
die Brille	pair of glasses
die Dame	lady
die Familie	family
die Frau	woman
die Freundschaft	friendship
die Geburt	birth
die Glatze	bald head
die Großmutter	grandmother
die Hausnummer	house number
die Katze	cat
die Kusine	cousin (female)
die Maus	mouse
die Mutter	mother
Mutti	mummy
die Nase	nose
die Oma/Omi	grandma
die Ratte	rat
die Schwester	sister
die Staatsangehörigkeit	nationality
die Stiefmutter	step-mother
die Tante	aunt
die Telefonnummer	telephone number
die Tochter	daughter
die Verwandschaft	relations
das Auge	eye
das Einzelkind	only child
das Fräulein	young lady
das Haar	hair

das Haustier	pet	groß	big, tall
das Kaninchen	rabbit	hässlich	ugly
das Kind	child	hell	light
das Leben	life	hübsch	pretty
das Mädchen	girl	jung	young
das Meerschweinchen	guineapig	klein	small
		kurz	short
das Pferd	horse	lang	long
das Taschengeld	pocket money	ledig	single
das Tier	animal	mittelgroß	of medium height

die Eltern	parents	schlank	slim
die Geschwister	brothers and sisters	schön	beautiful
		schwach	weak
die Großeltern	grandparents	stark	strong
		tot	dead
		verheiratet	married

aussehen	to look (appearance)
beschreiben	to describe
buchstabieren	to spell
hassen	to hate
heißen	to be called
wohnen	to live

alt	old
blond	blond
dick	fat
dunkel	dark
geboren	born
geschieden	divorced
gestorben	dead
getrennt	separated

1 Self, family and friends

1 Which word is the odd one out? Also, in each group, write another word that <u>does</u> belong in the group.

a Hund   Katze   Meerschweinchen   Onkel   Pferd   _____

b Bruder   Haustier   Schwester   Mutter   Tante   _____

c getrennt   geschieden   ledig   hässlich   verheiratet   _____

d Tante   Brille   Bart   Auge   Glatze   _____

e Oma   Mutter   Sohn   Kusine   Frau   _____

2 Complete the table.

Masculine	Feminine
Der Großvater	
	Die Schwester
Der Onkel	
Der Sohn	
	Die Kusine

3 Complete these star puzzles.

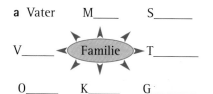
a Vater   M____   S_____
V_____   Familie   T_____
O_____   K_____   G_____

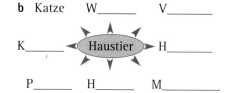
b Katze   W_____   V_____
K_____   Haustier   H_____
P_____   H_____   M_____

4 Write in the consonants to complete these words.

a _ a a _

b _ _ e u _ _

c _ e _ u _ _ _ _ _ a _

d _ a _ _ _ e _ _ e _ _

e E _ _ a _ _ _ e _ e

5 Write down the opposites.

alt _____   schön _____

dick _____   lang _____

schwach _____   hell _____

6 Complete the family tree.

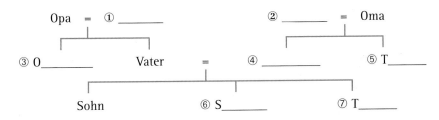

Opa = ① _____   ② _____ = Oma

③ O_____   Vater = ④ _____   ⑤ T_____

Sohn   ⑥ S_____   ⑦ T_____

7 Put the words into the correct columns.

Körper	Haustier	Familie

der Bart   der Vetter   das Kaninchen   die Glatze   das Auge
die Geschwister   der Hund   das Haar   die Nase
das Meerschweinchen   der Zwilling   die Ratte   der Erwachsene
die Großeltern   der Wellensittich

8 Solve the anagrams and give the English meaning.

legrotmißt   nerbistaeuchb   truGeb   rafitSevet   revtheraite

der Bahnhof	railway station	der Stadtrand	edge of town
der Bahnübergang	level crossing*	der Stall	stable*
der Bauernhof	farm	der Sturm	storm*
der Blitz	lightning*	der Weg	small road, path, trail*
der Brunnen	well, fountain		
der Dom	cathedral	der Wetterbericht	weather forecast
der Donner	thunder*	der Wind	wind
der Dunst	mist*		
der Einwohner	inhabitant	die Aufheiterung	brightening up
der Fluss	river*	die Brücke	bridge
der Frost	frost*	die Burg	castle
der Fußgänger	pedestrian	die Fußgängerzone	pedestrian precinct*
der Hagel	hail*		
der Himmel	sky, heaven	die Gegend	area
der Hügel	hill	die Hitze	heat*
der Jugendklub	youth club	die Jahreszeit	season
der Markt	market	die Karte	map
der Marktplatz	market place	die Kirche	church
der Nebel	fog	die Kreuzung	crossroads*
der Obstgarten	orchard*	die Kuh	cow
der Ort	place	die Kurve	bend in road*
der Park	park	die Nähe	vicinity, neighbourhood
der Pfad	path, small road, trail*		
		die Sonne	sun
der Platz	square	die Stadt	town
der Regen	rain	die Stadtmitte	town centre
der Schatten	shade*	die Vorstadt	suburb
der Schauer	shower	die Wettervorhersage	weather forecast
der Schnee	snow		
der Sonnenaufgang	sunrise*	die Wolke	cloud
der Sonnenschein	sunshine		
der Sonnenuntergang	sunset*	das Dorf	village
der Spielplatz	play area	das Einkaufszentrum	shopping centre

das Feld	field*	bedeckt	covered
das Freibad	open-air swimming pool	bewölkt	overcast
		dunstig	misty*
das Gebäude	building*	feucht	damp*
das Gewitter	storm*	heiß	hot
das Kino	cinema	hitzefrei	school closed (hot weather)
das Klima	climate	kalt	cold
das Krankenhaus	hospital	kühl	cool
das Land	land	mild	mild*
das Museum	museum	nass	wet
das Rathaus	town hall	neblig	foggy
das Schaf	sheep	regnerisch	rainy
das Schloss	castle	schwül	sultry, close*
das Schwimmbad	swimming pool	sonnig	sunny
		stürmisch	stormy*
das Stadion	stadium	trocken	dry
das Theater	theatre	von ... umgeben	surrounded by ...
das Wetter	weather		
das Wohngebiet	built-up area*	warm	warm
das Zentrum	centre	windig	windy
		wolkenlos	cloudless*
aufklären	to brighten up*	wolkig	cloudy
blitzen	there is lightning	Grad	degrees
donnern	to thunder*	Höchsttemperatur	highest temperature
frieren	to freeze	Tiefsttemperatur	lowest temperature
kalt werden	to get cold (weather)		
regnen	to rain		
scheinen	to shine*		
schneien	to snow		

1 What is the weather like?

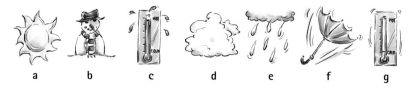

a   b   c   d   e   f   g

2 Write down the names of these buildings. Don't forget the genders!

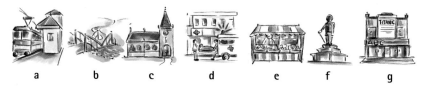

a   b   c   d   e   f   g

3 What is in this picture? Write down the words.

4 Put the words below into the correct columns.

Stadt	Land	Wetter

> das Dorf   der Schauer   der Dom   die Fußgängerzone
> das Wohngebiet   schwül   das Gewitter   der Hügel   das Krankenhaus
> der Fluss   der Donner   das Theater   der Blitz   das Schaf   das Feld

5 All these words have been split into two. **Put the halves back together.**

Jugend   zentrum   übergang   Sonnen   vorhersage   haus
Bahn   klub   bad   Kranken   temperatur   aufgang
Einkaufs   Schwimm   Höchst   Wetter

6 Write down the opposites.

heiß _____   bewölkt _____

kühl _____   Sonnenaufgang _____

nass _____

7 Where might you see these signs? Answer in German.

a **Nur für Fußgänger**   e **Schwimmen: nur im Sommer**

b **zu den Zügen**   f **Heute: _Hamlet_**

c **Spielplatz nur für Kinder**   g **Heute Abend: Disko**

d **Einfahrt nur für Krankenwagen**

8 Complete the sentences.

a Es gibt eine Brücke über dem _____.

b Die Stadt hat fünfzigtausend _____.

c Keine Schule heute: Wir haben _____.

d Es gibt viele Kühe auf dem _____.

e Wir wohnen nicht in der Stadt, sondern in einem _____.

f Es gibt einen guten Film im _____.

g Im Winter haben wir immer viel _____.

h Mein Haus ist in der _____ von dem Stadion.

der Bleistift	pencil	Naturwissenschaft	science
der Direktor	head teacher	die Pause	break
		die Probeprüfung	mock exam*
der Fehler	mistake	die Prüfung	exam*
der Fortschritt	progress	die Realschule	secondary school
der Gang	corridor*		
der Kassettenrekorder	cassette recorder*	die Regel	rule
der Kugelschreiber	biro	die Schule	school
der Kuli	biro	die Seite	page
der Lehrer	teacher	die Sozialkunde	sociology
der Leser	reader*	die Stunde	lesson
der Primaner	sixth former	die Turnhalle	gym
der Radiergummi	rubber	die Uniform	uniform
der Realschulabschluss	GCSE (equivalent)*	die Unterprima	lower sixth
		die Verbesserung	correction
der Schuldirektor	head teacher		
der Schüler	pupil	das Blatt	sheet of paper
der Schulhof	school playground	das Buch	book
		das Etui	pencil case*
der Schulleiter	headteacher*	das Fach	subject
der Stundenplan	timetable	das Federmäppchen	pencil case*
der Unterricht	lessons	das Gymnasium	grammar school
		das Heft	exercise book
die Arbeit	task/ assignment*	das Internat	boarding school*
		das Klassenzimmer	classroom
die Aufgabe	exercise	das Labor	laboratory
die Bibliothek	library	das Lieblingsfach	favourite subject
die Grundschule	primary school		
die Hauptschule	secondary modern school	das Lineal	ruler
		das Papier	paper
die Hauswirtschaft	home economics	das Pflichtfach	compulsory subject*
die Kantine	dining room		
die Klassenarbeit	class test*	das Semester	semester
die Mittagspause	lunch break		
die			

das Wörterbuch	dictionary	singen	to sing
das Zeugnis	report, diploma	unterrichten	to teach
		zeichnen	to draw
		zuhören	to listen
die Ferien	holidays		
die Hausaufgaben	homework	gemischt	mixed*
die Qualifikationen	qualifications	leicht	easy
		mündlich	oral
abschreiben	to copy out	obligatorisch	compulsory*
(ein Fach) abwählen	to drop (a subject)*	qualifiziert	qualified
		schulfrei	no school
anfangen	to start	schwer	difficult
antworten	to answer	streng	strict*
(ein Fach) aufgeben	to drop (a subject)*		
(die Schule) besuchen	to attend (school)*	Biologie	biology
		Chemie	chemistry
dauern	to last	Deutsch	German
enden	to finish	Drama	drama
erklären	to explain	Englisch	English
fehlen	to be absent	Erdkunde	geography
fragen	to ask	Französisch	French
korrigieren	to correct	Geschichte	history
lehren	to teach	Informatik	information technology
lernen	to learn		
(ein Experiment) machen	to do (an experiment)*	Kunst	art
		Mathe(matik)	maths
malen	to paint	Musik	music
mogeln	to cheat*	Physik	physics
nachsitzen	to stay in	Religion	R.E.
pauken	to revise*	Spanisch	Spanish
pfuschen	to do sloppy work*	Turnen	P.E.
		Werken	design and technology
schummeln	to cheat*		
schwänzen	to skive*		

1 Sort these words into the right groups.

Fächer	Sachen	Zimmer	Personen

Erdkunde   Schüler   Labor   Geschichte   Schuldirektor   Buch   Heft
Kunst   Bleistift   Turnhalle   Kantine   Lehrer   Werken   Ordner
Informatik   Primaner   Lineal   Turnen   Klassenzimmer   Bibliothek

2 Write down the name of the subject.

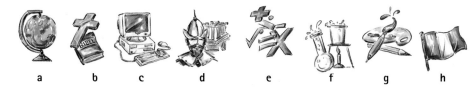

a   b   c   d   e   f   g   h

3 Fill in the gaps in these sentences.

a In meiner Schule gibt es mehr als tausend _____.

b Die Naturwissenschaften, also _____, _____, und
_____ sind meine Lieblingsfächer.

c Im Moment gehe ich nicht zur Schule. Wir haben sechs Wochen _____.

d Ich kann heute Abend nicht ausgehen. Ich muss die _____
machen.

e Mein Bruder ist sieben Jahre alt. Er ist in der _____ .

f In der Schule bekomme ich das Mittagessen in der _____.

g In _____ müssen wir viele neue Wörter lernen.

4 What is in the schoolbag?

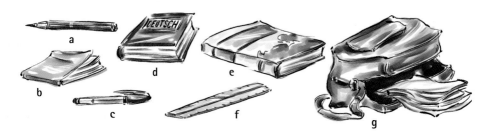

5 Find the pairs in this list of words.

Informatik	das Labor	die Bibliothek	Turnen	das Wörterbuch
Mathematik	die Prüfung	das Lineal	der Computer	Französisch
	die Turnhalle	das Buch	Chemie	pauken

6 What word would be a definition for each sentence?

a Diese Schule ist für die intelligentesten Schüler und Schülerinnen.

b Hier kann ich sehen, was die nächste Stunde ist.

c In diesem Zimmer spielen wir Basketball, Tischtennis usw.

d Das ist für die Eltern am Ende des Schuljahres.

e Eine Gruppe von Schülern fährt in eine andere Stadt oder ein anderes Land.

f Die Arbeit, die man zu Hause machen muss.

7 Find the two halves which go together to form a word.

Kassetten	Kugel	Haupt	Stunden	Lieblings	Wörter
	Schul	Mittags	Turn	Haus	

halle	plan	aufgaben	direktor	schreiber	schule	rekorder
		buch	fach	pause		

Education

der Arzt	doctor
der Beruf	job, career
der Berufsberater	careers advisor
der Erfolg	success
der Lebenslauf	C.V.
der Lehrling	apprentice
der Student	student
der Tierarzt	vet

die Abschlussprüfung	leaving/final exam
die Ausbildung	education, training
die Berufsausbildung	vocational training*
die Bildung	education
die Erziehung	education
die Lehre	apprenticeship
die Leistung	achievement
die Mittlere Reife	leaving exam (GCSE)*
die Oberstufe	upper school, sixth form
die Prüfung	test*
die Stufe	level, stage*
die Uni	university
die Universität	university
die Zukunft	future

das Abitur	school leaving exam

das Gehalt	salary
das Studium	study

bestehen	to pass exam*
durchfallen	to fail exam
heiraten	to marry
studieren	to study

berufstätig	employed
reich	rich

Work

der Arbeiter	employee
der Arbeitgeber	employer
der Arbeitnehmer	employee
der Bäcker	baker
der Bauer	builder
der Bauunternehmer	building contractor
der Beamte	civil servant*
der Berater	adviser
der Briefträger	postman
der Buchhalter	accountant
der Chef	boss
der Designer	designer*
der Elektriker	electrician
der Feierabend	end of work, closing time
der Geschäftsmann	businessman
der Informatiker	computer scientist

der Journalist	journalist		die Krankenschwester	nurse
der Kassierer	cashier		die Nachricht	news, item of information
der Kaufmann	businessman			
der Klempner	plumber		die Sekretärin	secretary
der Koch	cook		die Stelle	post, position, job
der Krankenpfleger	male nurse			
der Landarbeiter	farm worker*		die Stellenanzeige	job advertisement
der Landwirt	farmer*			
der Lohn	wages, pay*		das Arbeitspraktikum	work experience
der Manager	manager			
der Mechaniker	mechanic		das Berufspraktikum	job training
der Musiker	musician		das Büro	office
der Politiker	politician		das Vorstellungsgespräch	interview
der Polizist	policeman			
der Soldat	soldier			
der Teilzeitjob	part-time job		arbeiten	to work
der Verkäufer	sales assistant		austragen	to deliver (newspapers)
der Vertreter	representative			
der Weinbauer	vine grower*		Erfahrung sammeln	to gain experience*
der Zahnarzt	dentist			
			kopieren	to copy*
die Arbeit	work		sparen	to save
die Fabrik	factory		tippen	to type
die Firma	firm		verdienen	to earn
die Geschäftsfrau	business-woman			
die Hausfrau	housewife		am Apparat	on the telephone
die Industrie	industry		arbeitslos	out of work
die Kaffeepause	coffee break		Diplom-	qualified
die Kauffrau	business-woman		erfahren	experienced*
die Köchin	cook		schlecht bezahlt	badly paid

4   Future: Education and Work

Education

1 Put these words into chronological order.

das Abitur   der Beruf   bestehen   die Oberstufe
die Schule   das Vorstellungsgespräch   studieren

2 Complete this star puzzle.

M _____   A _____   Q _____

d _____   ◄ die Prüfung ►   b _____

s _____   E _____

3 Complete the words by adding to the start letters. Give three words every time.

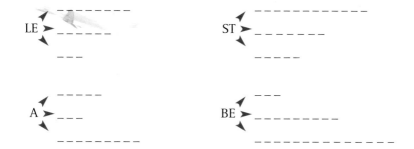

LE ► _ _ _ _ _ _ _ _
  _ _ _ _ _ _
  _ _ _

ST ► _ _ _ _ _ _ _ _ _ _
  _ _ _ _ _ _ _
  _ _ _ _

A ► _ _ _ _ _
  _ _ _
  _ _ _ _ _ _ _ _

BE ► _ _ _
  _ _ _ _ _ _ _ _
  _ _ _ _ _ _ _ _ _ _ _

4 Fill in the missing consonants in these words.

a   _ i e _ a _ _ _

b   _ u _ u _ _ _

c   _ e _ _ _ i _ _

d   _ e i e _ _ b _ _ d

e   A u _ _ i _ _ u _ _

f   _ _ u _ i e _ e _

Work

1 Which job is suggested by these pictures?

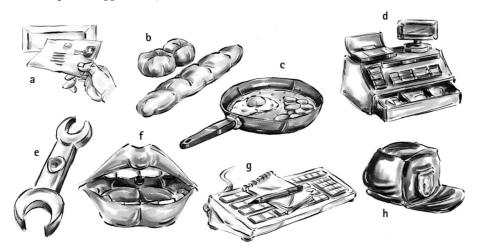

2 What job is being described here?

a Ich schreibe Zeitungsartikel.

b Ich repariere Autos.

c Ich arbeite im Flugzeug.

d Ich arbeite im Krankenhaus.

e Ich arbeite bei der Post.

f Ich arbeite im Supermarkt.

g Ich arbeite zu Hause.

h Ich arbeite im Büro.

3 Write down:

a three jobs beginning with K;

b three places of work;

c four jobs beginning with B.

4 All these words have been split into two. Put the halves back together.

Arbeit	arbeits	Arbeits	Brief	frau	geber	Haus	job	Kauf
Kranken	los	pfleger	praktikum	mann	Teilzeit	träger		

der Anschluss	connection	der Zug	train
der Auspuff	exhaust*	der Zuschlag	supplement
der Ausweis	identity card		
der Autobus	bus	die Abfahrt	departure
der Bus	bus	die Ankunft	arrival
der Busfahrer	bus driver	die Ausfahrt	exit (from
der Busbahnhof	bus station		garage, etc.)
der Fahrer	driver	die Autobahn	motorway
der Fahrplan	timetable	die Bundesstraße	federal road
der Flughafen	airport	die Bushaltestelle	bus stop
der Führerschein	driving licence	die Einzelfahrkarte	single ticket
der Gepäckträger	porter	die Eisenbahn	railway, train
	(luggage)*	die Fahrbahn	track, lane or
der Kofferraum	boot (of car)*		road*
der Kontrolleur	ticket	die Fahrkarte	ticket
	inspector	die Fahrt	journey
der Luftsteward(ess)	cabin steward	die Gepäckablage	luggage rack*
der Motor	engine	die Gepäck-	left luggage
der Parkplatz	car park,	aufbewahrungsstelle	office
	parking space	die Geschwindigkeit	speed*
der Pass	passport	die Heimfahrt	journey home*
der Rastplatz	picnic area	die Höchst-	maximum
	(roadside)*	geschwindigkeit	speed
der Reifen	tyre	die Landung	landing
der Reisende	traveller		(plane)*
der Schalter	ticket window	die Maut	toll*
der Scheinwerfer	headlight*	die Mautstelle	toll booth*
der Schlafwagen	sleeping car	die Panne	breakdown,
der Sitzplatz	seat (of a		puncture
	car)*	die Ringstraße	ring road*
der Stau	traffic jam	die Rückfahrkarte	return ticket
der Verkehr	traffic		
der Wagen	car	die Schiene	rail track*
der Wartesaal	waiting room*	die Spur	track, lane (of
			road)*

die Stoßzeit	rush hour*	bremsen	to brake
die U-Bahn	underground	einsteigen	to get on
die Umgebung	surroundings*	erreichen	to reach
die Umleitung	diversion*	fahren	to go (by vehicle)
die Windschutzscheibe	windscreen*	fliegen	to fly
		kommen	to come
das Abteil	compartment	kontrollieren	to check (tickets)
das Auto	car	landen	to land (plane)
das Benzin	petrol	mitfahren	to travel with, accompany
das Fahrrad	bicycle		
das Flugzeug	plane	parken	to park
das Gepäck	luggage	überholen	to overtake*
das Gleis	track, platform	umsteigen	to change (train, etc.)
das Luftkissenfahrzeug	hovercraft	verpassen	to miss (train, bus)
das Motorboot	motor boat*		
das Öl	oil	verzollen	to declare (at customs)
das Parken	parking*		
das Schild	sign, notice*	zurückkommen	to come back
das Zweirad	bicycle*		
		bleifrei	lead-free
die Bauarbeiten	roadworks*	Einfahrt verboten	no entry*
öffentliche Verkehrsmittel	public transport	früh	early
		Gute Reise!	Have a good journey!
abbiegen	to turn off	spät	late
abfahren	to depart	Verspätung haben	to be late
abfliegen	to take off	zu Fuß	on foot
an Bord gehen	to board (plane/boat)*		
ankommen	to arrive		
aufhalten	to delay*		
aussteigen	to get off		

1 Jigsaw words. **Make up eight words from these parts of words. Each word has three parts.**

> bahn Bus Bus Einzel fahr fahr fahrzeug halte hof karte karte
> kissen Luft Rück schutz scheibe stelle Wind

2 Put the words into the correct column.

Auto	Zug	Flugzeug

> die Bundesstraße fliegen die Ringstraße der Flughafen der Schlafwagen
> der Kofferraum landen das Gleis der Stau der Kontrolleur der Luftsteward
> die Landung überholen der Wartesaal der Zuschlag

3 Label these pictures.

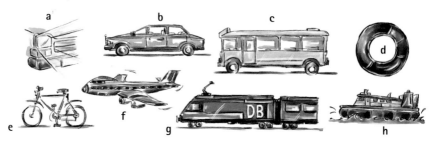

4 Put these verbs in the order that they would occur if you were on a journey.

> abfahren ankommen aussteigen einsteigen
> fahren überholen zurückkommen

5 Write down:

  a two words ending with 'platz'

  b three words ending with 'bahn'

  c three words ending with 'fahrt'

6 Add a part to the front of these words to make another word.

  a Schein   **b** Plan   **c** Fahrkarte   **d** Bahnhof   **e** Zeit
  f Rad   **g** Bus   **h** Hafen

7 Fill in the gaps in these sentences.

  a Der Zug hat fünf Minuten _____.

  b Der Zug kommt in zwanzig Minuten. Wir können in dem
     _____ sitzen.

  c Ich bin 17 Jahre alt. Ich darf einen _____ haben.

  d Das Gepäck ist in dem _____ von dem Auto.

  e Ich fahre nicht sehr oft in die Stadt. Ich kann nie einen
     _____ finden.

  f Die Autos stehen auf der Autobahn. Es gibt einen _____.

  g Wir fliegen um 4 Uhr. Wir müssen um 2 Uhr am _____ sein.

  h Ich fahre nicht gern. Ich gehe lieber _____ _____.

8 Complete the words by adding to the letters given. Give three words every time.

FAHR ⟩ — —
        _ _ _ _
        _ _ _ _ _

GEP ⟩ — — —
       _ _ _ _ _ _ _ _
       _ _ _ _ _ _ _ _ _ _ _ _ _ _ _ _ _ _

AUS ⟩ — — — —
       _ _ _ _
       _ _ _ _

der Aufenthalt	stay
der Ausflug	excursion
der Balkon	balcony
der Berg	mountain
der Blick	view
der Ferienjob	holiday job
der Hafen	port
der Jahrmarkt	funfair*
der Koffer	suitcase
der Picknickplatz	picnic area*
der Reiseleiter	tour leader*
der Rettungs-schwimmer	lifeguard*
der Ruhetag	closing day
der Sand	sand
der See	lake
der Sessellift	chair lift*
der Skilift	ski lift*
der Stadtteil	district*
der Strand	beach
der Teil	part, district
der Tiergarten	zoo
der Tourist	tourist
der Turm	tower
der Urlaub	holiday, vacation
der Urlauber	holidaymaker*
der Yachthafen	yacht marina*

die Auskunft	information
die Broschüre	brochure
die Fremdsprache	foreign language
die Führung	conducted tour
die Gastfamilie	host family
die Gastfreundschaft	hospitality
die Grenze	border, frontier
die Information	information
die Insel	island
die Küste	coast
die Landschaft	scenery
die Partnerstadt	twin town
die Pauschalreise	package holiday*
die Reise	journey
die Rundfahrt	tour
die See	sea
die Seilbahn	cable car*
die Sehenswürdigkeit	sight
die Sesselbahn	chair lift*
die Sonnenbrille	sunglasses
die Sonnencreme	sun cream
die Stadtrundfahrt	tour of town
die Terrasse	terrace
die Tour	tour
die Wiese	field, meadow*
die Überfahrt	(sea) crossing*
das Boot	boat
das Gebiet	area*
das Gebirge	mountains
das Land	country

das Meer	sea	Winterurlaub machen	to go on a winter holiday*
das Reisebüro	travel agent's		
das Schiff	ship		
das Stadtviertel	area of town*	an der Küste	on the coast
das Touristenbüro	tourist office	an der See	by the sea
das Trinkgeld	tip	auf dem Lande	in the country
das Verkehrsamt	tourist office	historisch	historical
das Ziel	goal, destination	malerisch	picturesque
		östlich	east(ern)*
das Zuhause	home*	Schönen Aufenthalt!	Have a nice stay!
		seekrank	seasick*
die Betriebsferien	annual closing*	städtisch	urban*
die Ferien	holidays	westlich	west(ern)*
die Sommerferien	summer holidays		

anschauen	to look at
auspacken	to unpack
beilegen	to enclose
besichtigen	to view, sightsee
buchen	to book
bummeln	to stroll
erfahren	to learn, find out, experience
mieten	to hire, rent
packen	to pack
planen	to plan
reservieren	to reserve
(sich) sonnen	to sunbathe

1 Find synonyms for the following words.

a die Stadttour _____ **d** reservieren _____

b die Fahrt _____ **e** das Informationsbüro _____

c die See _____ **f** die Ferien _____

2 Put the words into the correct columns.

Landschaft	Tour	Person

der Berg   besichtigen   der Urlauber   die Insel   die Küste
die Pauschalreise   der Reiseleiter   der See   die Sehenswürdigkeit
die Stadtrundfahrt   der Strand   der Tourist   der Turm
der Rettungsschwimmer

3 Fill in the missing words on this postcard.

Schöne Grüße aus dem Urlaub!

Unser Hotel liegt an der (a) _____ .

Der (b) _____ aus dem Hotelfenster ist sehr schön. Das Wetter ist
auch sehr schön: Wir sitzen jeden Tag am (c)_____ und
(d)_____ _____ . Abends sitzen wir auf dem (e)_____.
Wir haben viele (f)_____ gemacht und der (g)_____ hat
viele Informationen gegeben.

Ich habe den Urlaub im Reisebüro (h)_____ und ich habe einige
(i)_____ vom Verkehrsamt bekommen.

4 Match the correct halves of these sentences.

a Die Überfahrt war sehr stürmisch,

b Der Blick aus dem Fenster ist schön:

c Wir haben eine Stadtrundfahrt gemacht

d Italien ist ein schönes Land:

e Ich habe in den Broschüren gelesen,

1 Es hat viele Sehenswürdigkeiten.

2 dass der Turm in der Stadtmitte sehr malerisch ist.

3 und wir haben einen Weinberg besucht.

4 und ich war seekrank.

5 Wir können das Meer sehen.

5 Label this picture.

der Aufzug	lift	die Vollpension	full board
der Balkon	balcony	die Zahnbürste	toothbrush
der Campingplatz	camp site	die Zahnpasta	toothpaste
der Eingang	entrance		
der Empfang	reception	das Doppelzimmer	double room
der Fernseher	TV set	das Einzelzimmer	single room
der Gang	corridor	das Frühstück	breakfast
der Lift	lift	das Gasthaus	pub
der Mieter	tenant*	das Hotel	hotel
der Pförtner	porter (hotel)*	das Waschbecken	wash basin
der Platz	space*	das WC	toilet, WC
der Rasierapparat	electric shaver	das Zelt	tent
der Schlafsack	sleeping bag	das Zimmer	room
der Schlüssel	key		
der Speisesaal	dining room	Unterkunft und Verpflegung	board and lodgings
der Wohnwagen	caravan		
die Abreise	departure	bleiben	to stay
die Dusche	shower	buchen	to book
die Ferienwohnung	holiday home*	reservieren	to reserve
die Halbpension	half board	übernachten	to stay overnight
die Jugendherberge	youth hostel		
die Luftmatratze	air bed*	unterbringen	to accommodate*
die Nacht	night		
die Pension	boarding house	zelten	to camp
die Reservierung	reservation		
die Rezeption	reception	besetzt	occupied, full
die Seife	soap	frei	free
die Sozialwohnung	council housing*	inklusive	inclusive
		luxuriös	luxurious
die Tageszeitung	daily newspaper	möbliert	furnished
		unbequem	uncomfortable
die Übernachtung	overnight stay	unbesetzt	unoccupied
die Unterkunft	board		

1 Write down the names of these items.

    a   b   c   d   e   f   g

2 With what do you connect these words? Write C for the campsite, H for the hotel and B for both.

a der Balkon   b der Schlafsack   c die Dusche   d Halbpension
e der Schlüssel   f der Empfang   g die Übernachtung   h das Zelt
i das Doppelzimmer   j das Waschbecken   k die Luftmatratze

3 a Write down two words for 'lift'.
  b Write down two words ending with –zimmer.
  c Write down two words for 'reception'.

4 These words have all been split into two. Match up the two halves.

apparat	becken	Auf	Wohn	herberge	Jugend	kunft	pension
platz	Rasier	zug	wagen	Unter	Voll	Wasch	Zelt

5 Complete these words by adding to the letters given. Give three words every time.

6 Correct the following sentences.

a Wir zelten in der Jugendherberge.

b Wir bekommen Vollpension: Frühstück und Abendessen.

c Wir essen in dem Aufzug im Hotel.

d Mein Bruder und ich schlafen in einem Einzelzimmer.

der Amerikaner	American	die Französin	Frenchwoman
der Brieffreund	pen friend	die Niederlande	Netherlands
der Belgier	Belgian	die Nordsee	North Sea
der Däne	Dane	die Ostsee	Baltic Sea
der Deutsche	German	die Person	person
der Engländer	Englishman	die Schweiz	Switzerland
der Franzose	Frenchman	die Türkei	Turkey
der Fremde	foreigner		
der Grieche	Greek	das Ausland	foreign countries
der Holländer	Dutchman		
der Ire	Irishman	das Mittelmeer	Mediterranean
der Italiener	Italian		
der Kanal	English Channel	die Alpen	the Alps
der Norden	north	die Leute	people
der Norweger	Norwegian	die USA	USA
der Osten	east		
der Österreicher	Austrian	Afrika	Africa
der Pole	Pole	Amerika	America
der Portugiese	Portugese	Bayern	Bavaria
der Rhein	River Rhine	Belgien	Belgium
der Russe	Russian	Dänemark	Denmark
der Schotte	Scot	Deutschland	Germany
der Schweizer	Swiss	England	England
der Spanier	Spaniard	Europa	Europe
der Süden	south	Frankreich	France
der Türke	Turk	Griechenland	Greece
der Westen	west	Großbritannien	Great Britain
		Irland	Ireland
die Donau	River Danube	Italien	Italy
die Engländerin	Englishwoman	Köln	Cologne
die EU	European Union	München	Munich

Norwegen	Norway	schwedisch	Swedish
Österreich	Austria	schweizerisch	Swiss
Polen	Poland	spanisch	Spanish
Russland	Russia	türkisch	Turkish
Schottland	Scotland	walisisch	Welsh
Schweden	Sweden		
Spanien	Spain		
Wales	Wales		
Wien	Vienna		

im Ausland	abroad
ins Ausland fahren	to go abroad

amerikanisch	American
belgisch	Belgian
britisch	British
dänisch	Danish
deutsch	German
englisch	English
französisch	French
fremd	foreign
griechisch	Greek
holländisch	Dutch
irisch	Irish
italienisch	Italian
norwegisch	Norwegian
österreichisch	Austrian
polnisch	Polish
portugiesisch	Portugese
russisch	Russian
schottisch	Scottish

1 Where are these capital cities? Write down the country.

a London   d Washington   g Edinburg   i Madrid
b Paris   e Rom   h Wien   j Berlin
c Athen   f Brüssel

2 Complete the table.

England	englisch	
	deutsch	
Frankreich		
Italien		der Italiener
	griechisch	
		der Spanier
		der Türke
		der Schweizer

3 Which language is this? Write it down in German.

a Good morning!   c Guten Tag!   e Buenos dias!   g Lyi günler!
b Bonjour!   d Buongiorno! f Kalimera!   h Bom dia!

4 Label this map.

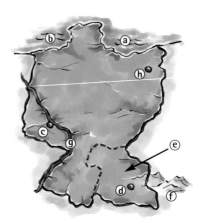

5 Wie heißt/heißen. . .

a das Meer zwischen Deutschland und Skandinavien?

b die See zwischen Deutschland und England?

c das Wasser zwischen Belgien/Frankreich und England?

d die Hauptstadt von Österreich?

e das Meer zwischen Europa und Afrika?

f ein Land in Europa mit vier Sprachen?

g die Berge in Süddeutschland und Österreich?

6 Which countries do cars with these registration plates come from?

7 In which country can you see the following sights?

| a | b | c | d | e |

8 Solve the anagrams.

a denfreiBurf

b ide aonuD

c cheatislini

d edi Ndreose

e Banery

f zarFnose

g sad retiMeeltm

h opErau

Services

der Absender	sender
der Anruf	telephone call
der Brief	letter
der Briefkasten	letter box
der Euro	Euro
der Euroschein	Euro note
der Hörer	telephone receiver
der Kurs	exchange rate
der Reisescheck	traveller's cheque
der Wechsel	change, exchange

die Ansichtskarte	picture postcard
die Bank	bank
die Briefmarke	stamp
die E-Mail	e-mail
die Leerung	collection (post box)*
die letzte Leerung	last collection
die nächste Leerung	next collection
die Post	mail*
die Postkarte	postcard
die Telefonkarte	phone card*
die Telefonnummer	telephone number
die Telefonzelle	telephone box
die Vorwahlnummer	dialling code
die Wechselstube	bureau de change

das Fundbüro	lost property office
das Geld	money
das Kleingeld	small change
das Postamt	post office
das Telefonat	phone call

ausfüllen	to fill in
abschicken	to send off
anrufen	to telephone
einwerfen	to put money in
faxen	to fax
mailen	to send an e-mail
mieten	to rent, hire
nachsenden	to send on
einen Scheck einlösen	to cash a cheque*
schicken	to send
telefonieren	to telephone
verbinden	to connect
wählen	to dial
wechseln	to change

außer Betrieb	not working, out of order*
besetzt	engaged (phone)

Finding the Way

der Kilometer	kilometre
der Stadtplan	town plan
der Wegweiser	signpost

die Adresse	address
die Ampel	traffic lights
die Ecke	corner
die Einbahnstraße	one-way street
die Hauptstraße	main street
die Kreuzung	crossroads
die Landkarte	map
die Seite	side
die Straße	street

das Meter	metre
das Parkhaus	multi-storey car park
das Schild	sign

finden	to find
folgen	to follow
gehen	to go
lösen	to buy (ticket)
nehmen	to take
suchen	to look for
überqueren	to cross

dritte	third
drüben	over there
entlang	along

erste	first
gegenüber	opposite
geradeaus	straight on
hinauf	up
hinter	behind
hinunter	down
in der Nähe von	near to
letzte	last
links	left
mindestens	at least
nächste	next
neben	near to (next to)
rechts	right
um	around
ungefähr	approximately
vor	in front of
weit	far
zweite	second

auf der linken / rechten Seite	on the left- / right-hand side
Entschuldigen Sie	Excuse me
Entschuldigung!	Excuse me!
Wie komme ich am besten zum / zur / nach ...?	Where is / how do I get to ...?
wo	where

Services

1 Complete the words by adding to the letters given. Give three words each time.

POS ➤ _ _ _ _ _ _ _
_ _ _ _

TEL ➤ _ _ _ _ _ _ _ _
_ _ _ _ _ _ _ _
_ _ _ _ _ _ _ _ _ _

AN ➤ _ _ _
_ _ _ _ _ _ _ _ _ _
_ _ _ _ _

2 Write the German words for the following:

   a   b   c   d   e

3 Match the verb with the appropriate noun.

a der Kurs   **b** der Brief   **c** die E-Mail   **d** die Telefonzelle

| wählen | mailen | schicken | wechseln |

4 Put these phrases into the correct order. What activity are you doing here?

verbinden   sprechen   Auf Wiederhören sagen   den Hörer auflegen
Geld einwerfen   wählen   den Hörer abnehmen

5 Fill in the gaps in these sentences.

a Ich habe meinem Freund einen _____ geschrieben.

b Er hat auch einen Computer. Ich kann eine E-Mail _____.

c Im Urlaub habe ich meinen Freunden eine _____ geschickt.

d Ich muss telefonieren. Ist hier in der Nähe eine _____?

e Ich kann ohne Geld telefonieren. Ich habe eine _____.

Finding the Way

1 Write down the correct German word.

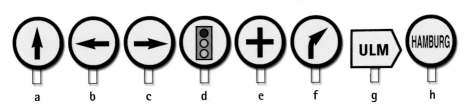

a   b   c   d   e   f   g   h

2 Write down the opposites.

a hinter _____   c erste _____

b links _____   d suchen _____

3 Fill in the missing words in this conversation.

a)_____! Ich b)_____ die Post. c)_____ ist sie, bitte? Ich kann
sie auf dem d)_____ nicht e)_____.

Die Post? Ja, f)_____ Sie hier g)_____. h)_____ Sie die
i)_____ Straße j)_____ . Die Post ist auf der k)_____ Seite. Es
ist l)_____ ein Kilometer von hier entfernt.

> erste   finden   gehen   geradeaus   Entschuldigung!   links
> nehmen   rechten   Stadtplan   suche   ungefähr   wo

4 Solve the anagrams.

a grunzKeu   e edgaresau

b tanSltapd   f kanteaLdr

c nequïrrbeeu   g sirWeeweg

d brasthEneißan

der Arm	arm	die Erste Hilfe	first aid*
der Arzt	doctor	die Füllung	filling (teeth)
der Bauch	stomach	die Gesundheit	health
der Chirurg	surgeon*	die Grippe	flu
der Daumen	thumb	die Hand	hand
der Durchfall	diarrhoea	die Hilfe	help
der Finger	finger	die Krankheit	illness
der Fuß	foot	die Lippe	lip
der Gips	plaster (for broken limb)	die Medizin	medicine
		die Niere	kidney*
der Hals	neck	die Panne	breakdown*
der Heuschnupfen	hay fever*	die Pille	pill, tablet
der Husten	cough*	die Polizei	police
der Kopf	head	die Polizeiwache	police station*
der Körper	body	die Praxis	doctor's surgery
der Magen	stomach	die Schulter	shoulder
der Mund	mouth	die Sicherheit	safety
der Notfall	emergency	die Sprechstunde	surgery, consulting hours
der Rücken	back		
der Schmerz	pain*	die Stimme	voice
der Schnupfen	cold	die Stirn	forehead*
der Sonnenbrand	sunburn*	die Tablette	tablet
der Sonnenstich	sunstroke*	die Temperatur	temperature
der Termin	appointment*	die Untersuchung	check-up*
der Unfall	accident	die Verbesserung	improvement*
der Verband	dressing*	die Werkstatt	workshop*
der Zahn	tooth	die Zehe	toe
		die Zunge	tongue
die Behandlung	treatment		
die Brust	chest, breast		
die Erkältung	cold		

das Aspirin	aspirin*	sich in den Finger schneiden	to cut one's finger*
das Bein	leg	sich übergeben	to be sick
das Blut	blood	untersuchen	to examine
das Fieber	fever*	sich die Hand verbrennen	to burn one's hand*
das Gesicht	face	verletzen	to injure
das Knie	knee	weh tun	to hurt
das Medikament	medicine		
das Ohr	ear		
das Pflaster	plaster	blass	pale
das Röntgenbild	x-ray*	gebrochen	broken
		gefunden	found
die Schmerzen	pains	gesund	healthy
		kaputt	broken
atmen	to breathe*	krank	ill
sich das Bein brechen	to break one's leg	ordentlich	tidy
brechen	to break	unordentlich	untidy
bremsen	to brake	verboten	forbidden
sich erbrechen	to be sick	verletzt	wounded
sich erholen	to recover	verstopft	constipated
sich erkälten	to catch a cold		
fallen	to fall	Achtung!	Watch out!
ein Formular ausfüllen	to fill in a form	Hilfe!	Help!*
sich fühlen	to feel	mir ist übel	I feel sick
sich krank fühlen	to feel ill	Vorsicht!	Watch out!
helfen	to help	Halsschmerzen	sore throat
husten	to cough	Kopfschmerzen	headache
leiden an	to suffer from	Magenschmerzen	stomach-ache
pflegen	to care for*	Ohrenschmerzen	earache
reparieren	to repair	Zahnschmerzen	toothache
röntgen	to x-ray*		

1 Label the parts of the body indicated.

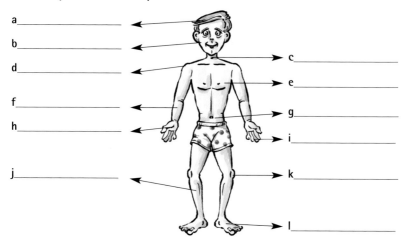

a_____

b_____

d_____

f_____

h_____

j_____

c_____

e_____

g_____

i_____

k_____

l_____

2 Label the parts of the head indicated.

a_____

c_____

e_____

b_____

d_____

f_____

g_____

3 Is the person ill (krank)? If so write K. Are they injured (verletzt)? Then write V. Or is it something dangerous (gefährlich)? Write G.

a Der Chirurg will an meinem Bein operieren.

b Ich habe mein Bein gebrochen.

c Ich muss ein Medikament nehmen.

d Ich muss alle fünf Minuten auf die Toilette gehen.

e Ich nehme zu viele Tabletten.

f Vorsicht! Hier kannst du fallen.

g Ich huste und ich habe eine Erkältung.

h Mein Arm tut weh.

i Du fährst zu schnell. Es kann einen Unfall geben.

4 Find the odd one out.

a Knie   Bein   Fuß   Hand   Fieber

b verletzt   verboten   verstopft   kaputt   krank

c Sonnenstich   Grippe   Tablette   Schnupfen   Erkältung

d blass   krank   husten   gesund   weh tun

5 What is wrong with the person? What have they injured? Write the correct German word.

a "Ich kann nicht schreiben."   e "Ich war zu lange in der Sonne."

b "Ich kann nicht sprechen."   f "Ich habe zu viel gegessen."

c "Ich kann nicht gehen."   g "Die Musik in der Disko war zu laut."

d "Ich kann nicht hören."

6 Find another way of saying these phrases.

a Ich habe einen Schnupfen.   d Ich habe eine sehr hohe Temperatur.

b Ich muss Pillen nehmen.   e Ich fühle mich krank.

c Achtung!

7 Sometimes German words are the same as the English word. There are four in this unit. What are they?

8 Sometimes the German and English words are very similar. Can you find ten from this unit?

der Baum	tree	der Vorhang	curtain
der Bungalow	bungalow	der Wecker	alarm clock
der CD-Spieler	CD player	der Wohnblock	block of flats
der Computer	computer		
der Dachboden	loft*	die Blume	flower
der Drucker	printer	die Decke	ceiling*
der Fernseher	TV set	die Diskette	disk, diskette
der Fußboden	floor	die Garage	garage
der Garten	garden	die Gardine	curtain
der Geschirr- spülautomat	dishwasher	die Heizung	heating
		die Küche	kitchen
der Herd	cooker	die Lampe	lamp
der Kamin	fireplace*	die Leiter	ladder*
der Keller	cellar*	die Mauer	(outside) wall
der Kühlschrank	fridge	die Mikrowelle	microwave*
der Mixer	blender	die Pflanze	plant
der Öffner	opener	die Putzfrau	cleaner
der Rasen	lawn*	die Software	software
der Putzmann	cleaner	die Steckdose	electric socket
der Schalter	switch	die Stereoanlage	stereo unit
der Schrank	cupboard	die Tapete	wallpaper
der Schreibtisch	desk	die Taschenlampe	torch
der Sessel	armchair	die Tiefkühltruhe	deep freeze
der Spiegel	mirror	die Toilette	toilet
der Stadtbewohner	city dweller*	die Treppe	stairs
der Stecker	plug*	die Tür	door
der Strom	electricity*	die Wand	wall
der Stuhl	chair	die Waschmaschine	washing machine
der Teppich	carpet		
der Teppichboden	carpeting	die Wohnung	flat
der Tisch	table	die Zentralheizung	central heating
der Treppenflur	landing*		

das Arbeitszimmer	study	das Zimmer	room
das Bad	bath		
das Badezimmer	bathroom	die Fensterläden	shutters*
das Bett	bed	die Möbel	furniture
das Bild	picture		
das Bügeleisen	iron*	begießen	to water
das Dach	roof	gießen	to pour, to water
das Doppelhaus	semi-detached house*	pflanzen	to plant
das Einfamilienhaus	detached house*	pflücken	to pick
		speichern	to store, save (data)
das Esszimmer	dining room		
das Federbett	duvet*	verschlafen	to oversleep
das Fenster	window		
das Gebäude	building	draußen	outside
das Gas	gas	drinnen	inside
das Gras	grass	oben	upstairs
das Haus	house	unten	downstairs
das Kopfkissen	cushion		
das Leck	leak*		
das Licht	light		
das Möbelstück	piece of furniture		
das Plumeau	duvet*		
das Poster	poster		
das Schlafzimmer	bedroom		
das Schloss	lock*		
das Spülbecken	sink (kitchen)*		
das Telefon	telephone		
das Tuch	cloth		
das Videogerät	video machine		
das Wohnzimmer	living room		

1 Put these things in the room they normally go in.

die Waschmaschine   das Bett   das Bad   der Kühlschrank   der Tisch
der Geschirrspülautomat   der Fernseher   das Auto   der Herd
der Sessel   der Kleiderschrank

a das Badezimmer   _____

b das Esszimmer   _____

c die Küche   _____ _____ _____ _____

d die Garage   _____

e das Schlafzimmer   _____ _____

f das Wohnzimmer   _____ _____

2 Write down the names of these objects. Include the gender!

3 Write down the names of these houses.

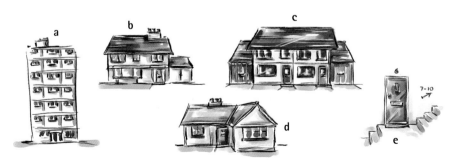

4 Write down words with these endings, giving the number of words asked for:

a Zwei mit ......haus

b Vier mit ......zimmer

c Drei mit ......ung

d Fünf mit ......er

5 Add another part to these words to make a new word. Then give the meaning of both words.

a die Tasche

b die Maschine

c das Haus

d das Zimmer

e das Dach

6 Here are some word definitions. What are the words?

a Er steht auf dem Tisch neben dem Bett.

b Ich sehe mich darin.

c Hier gehe ich von unten nach oben.

d Hier ,wohnt' das Auto.

e Man findet sie im Garten.

f Das Zimmer unter dem Haus.

g Tisch, Stuhl, Sessel, usw.

h Er hängt vor dem Fenster.

7 Where do you find these things in the house? Write down O for 'oben', U for 'unten', B for 'beide' and D for 'draußen'.

a das Badezimmer

b der Keller

c die Pflanze

d der Dachboden

e die Küche

f der Baum

g die Decke

h der Wecker

i der Teppich

8 Put these words in the order in which you would find them in the house, starting from the top of the house.

die Treppe	das Dach	das Schlafzimmer
der Kamin	der Keller	der Dachboden

der Umzug	house move*

die Gartenarbeit	gardening
die Kassette	cassette
die Mahlzeit	mealtime
die Mittagszeit	midday, lunchtime
die Musik	music

das Abendessen	evening meal
das Frühstück	breakfast
das Mittagessen	lunch
das Radio	radio

abräumen	to clear (table)*
abspülen	to wash up
abtrocknen	to dry up*
abwaschen	to wash up
anmachen	to turn on (light)
aufräumen	to tidy up
aufstehen	to get up
aufwachen	to wake up
ausmachen	to turn off (light)
ausstatten	to furnish, equip*
basteln	to do odd jobs, DIY
bügeln	to iron
decken	to set (the table)
(sich) duschen	to shower
einkaufen	to shop
essen	to eat
fernsehen	to watch TV

frühstücken	to have breakfast
heizen	to heat
herunterfahren	to shut down (computer)*
herunterladen	to download*
hören	to hear, listen
klingeln	to ring (alarm, doorbell)
klopfen	to knock*
kochen	to cook
lesen	to read
mähen	to mow
den Rasen mähen	to mow the lawn*
plaudern	to chat
putzen	to clean
(sich die Zähne) putzen	to clean one's teeth
(sich) rasieren	to have a shave
schlafen	to sleep
teilen	to share
trinken	to drink
üben	to practise
umziehen	to move house*
verlassen	to leave
waschen	to wash
(sich) waschen	to have a wash
wecken	to wake someone up

eigen	own*
zu Hause	at home

1 What are these people doing? Write down the verbs.

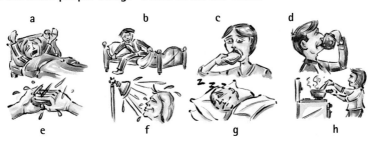

2 Put these sentences into the correct order.

a Ich dusche mich.

b Ich verlasse das Haus.

c Ich esse das Mittagessen.

d Ich wache auf.

e Der Wecker klingelt.

f Ich koche das Abendessen.

g Ich frühstücke.

h Ich stehe auf.

3 Where does this happen? Complete the table.

a Im Badezimmer	b Im Schlafzimmer	c In der Küche

Ich wache auf.   Ich trinke.   Ich dusche mich.   Ich schlafe.
Ich koche.   Der Wecker klingelt.   Ich esse.   Ich wasche mich.
Ich stehe auf.   Ich putze mir die Zähne.

4 When do you do this? Write V for 'vor dem Essen', N for 'nach dem Essen' and B for 'beim Essen'.

abräumen   kochen   abwaschen   decken   abspülen
essen   plaudern   abtrocknen

der Fotograf	photographer	das Feuerwerk	fireworks
der Friseur	hairdresser	das Geschenk	present
der Geburtstag	birthday	das Tonbandgerät	tape recorder
der Glückwunsch	congratulations		
der Lärm	noise*	ablehnen	to refuse*
der Neujahrstag	New Year's Day	annehmen	to accept
der Stollen	(German Christmas cake*)	danken	to thank
		einladen	to invite
der Umzug	procession*	feiern	to celebrate
		gratulieren	to congratulate
die Atmosphäre	atmosphere*	schenken	to give a present
die Ehe	marriage		
die Einladung	invitation	alles Gute	all the best
die Festhalle	hall (for a party)	dankbar	grateful, thankful
die Hochzeit	wedding	Frohe Weihnachten!	Happy Christmas!
die Party	party		
die Stimmung	atmosphere, mood	Ostern	Easter
		Pfingsten	Whit
die Verlobung	engagement	Silvester	New Year's Eve
die Videorekorder	video recorder	Weihnachten	Christmas

1 Write down the words suggested by these pictures.

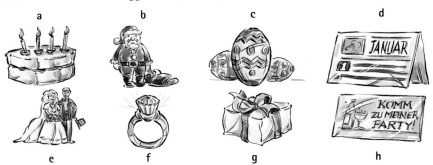

a   b   c   d

e   f   g   h

2 Fill in the gaps in these greetings.

  a Alles _____ zum Geburtstag.

  b Frohe _____!

  c Heute hast du Geburtstag? Ich _____!

3 Put these sentences into the correct chronological order.

  a Ich habe meinem Freund das Geschenk gegeben.

  b Ich bin zur Party gegangen.

  c Ich habe die Einladung angenommen.

  d Wir haben gut gefeiert.

  e Ich habe eine Einladung bekommen.

  f Er war sehr dankbar.

  g Ich habe ein Geschenk gekauft.

4 Fill in the missing consonants in these words.

  a _ e i _ _ a _ _ _ e _   **c** _ i _ _ e _ _ e _

  b _ _ i _ _ _ _ e _   **d** _ e _ u _ _ _ _ a _

5 Put these festivals into chronological order, starting on January 1st.

Weihnachten	Pfingsten	Silvester	Ostern	Neujahrstag

der Aschenbecher	ashtray*
der Raucher	smoker*
der Sportverein	sports club
der Stress	stress
der Tabak	tobacco
der Tennisplatz	tennis court
der Vegetarier	vegetarian
der Wanderer	hiker
der Zuschauer	spectator*

die Aktivität	activity
die Athletik	athletics
die Badewanne	bathtub*
die Bettdecke	blanket, quilt, duvet
die Droge	drug*
die Entspannung	relaxation*
die Haut	skin*
die Lunge	lung*
die Übung	practice
die Verschwendung	waste, wastefulness*
die Werbung	advertising

das Baden	bathing*
das Blut	blood*
das Mountainbike	mountain bike*
das Rauchen	smoking*
das Sportzentrum	sports centre
das Vorurteil	prejudice*

abnehmen	to lose weight
sich amüsieren	to enjoy oneself

atmen	to breathe
sich ausruhen	to rest
baden	to swim, have a bath
im Bett bleiben	to stay in bed
Diät machen	to go on a diet
Drogen probieren	to try drugs*
sich entspannen	to relax*
klettern	to climb
rauchen	to smoke
Spaß haben	to have fun
Sport treiben	to do sport
verschwenden	to waste*
windsurfen	to windsurf
zerstören	to destroy
zunehmen	to put on weight

allergisch gegen	allergic to*
bei guter Gesundheit	in good health*
bei schlechter Gesundheit	in bad health*
chemisch	chemical*
drogenabhängig	addicted to drugs
dünn	thin
gestresst	stressed*
langweilig	boring
relaxt	relaxed
schwindlig	dizzy

1 Are these people fit or unfit? Write F for fit, U for unfit.

   a Ich esse viel Gemüse.

   b Ich rauche eine Packung Zigaretten jeden Tag.

   c Ich gehe oft zum Sportzentrum.

   d Ich jogge jeden Tag zwanzig Minuten.

   e Ich esse kein fettiges Fleisch.

   f Ich gehe sehr oft wandern.

   g Ich bleibe oft zu Hause und sehe viel fern.

   h Ich habe in der letzten Zeit sehr viel zugenommen.

2 Solve the anagrams.

   a hekilAtt

   b hebmanne

   c griechalls

   e Wunbreg

   f greetraVi

   g poStnirever

3 Fill in the gaps in these sentences.

   a Ich rauche nicht. _____ ist ungesund.

   b Ich esse kein Fleisch. Ich bin _____.

   c Ich gehe oft zum _____. Fußball, Laufen, Tennis: ich mache alles.

   d Ich muss _____. Ich bin zu dick.

   e Ich arbeite zu viel. Ich muss _____ _____.

   f Mein Opa ist siebzig, aber er ist in _____ _____.

   g Du bist faul! Du bleibst bis zehn Uhr _____ _____.

der Apfel	apple	die Apfelsine	orange
der Apfelsaft	apple juice	die Aprikose	apricot
der Blumenkohl	cauliflower	die Banane	banana
der Essig	vinegar	die Birne	pear
der Fisch	fish	die Blätterteigpastete	vol-au-vent*
der Kaffee	coffee	die Bratwurst	grilled sausage
der Kakao	cocoa	die Butter	butter
der Käse	cheese	die Chips	crisps
der Kohl	cabbage	die Cola	cola
der Kuchen	cake	die Currywurst	curried sausage
der Lachs	salmon	die Erdbeere	strawberry
der Lebkuchen	gingerbread*	die Erbse	pea
der Orangensaft	orange juice	die Frucht	fruit
der Pfeffer	pepper	die Himbeere	raspberry
der Pfirsich	peach	die Kartoffel	potato
der Reis	rice	die Leber	liver*
der Rotkohl	red cabbage	die Leberwurst	liver sausage
der Rotwein	red wine	die Limonade	lemonade
der Saft	juice	die Marmelade	jam
der Salat	salad	die Milch	milk
der Sauerbraten	braised beef	die Nuss	nut
der Schinken	ham	die Orange	orange
der Schweinebraten	roast pork	die Pflaume	plum
der Senf	mustard	die Pommes frites	chips
der Speck	bacon	die Praline	chocolate (in box)
der Tee	tea		
der Wein	wine	die Sahne	cream
der Weißwein	white wine	die Scheibe	slice
der Zucker	sugar	die Schokolade	chocolate
		die Suppe	soup
		die Süßigkeit	sweet

die Tomate	tomato		das Rezept	recipe
die Torte	tart, cake		das Rindfleisch	beef
die Weintraube	grape		das Salz	salt
die Wurst	sausage		das Sauerkraut	pickled cabbage
die Zitrone	lemon		das Schweinefilet	filet of pork
die Zwiebel	onion		das Schweinefleisch	pork
			das Spiegelei	fried egg
das Bier	beer		das Wasser	water
das Brot	bread		das Würstchen	small sausage
das Brötchen	bread roll			
das Ei	egg		die Zutaten	ingredients
das Eis	ice-cream			
das Fleisch	meat		essen	to eat
das Gebäck	biscuits		fressen	to eat (animal), to guzzle (human)
das Gemüse	vegetable			
das Gericht	dish		mischen	to mix
das Getränk	drink		schneiden	to cut
das Hähnchen	chicken		trinken	to drink
das Kalbfleisch	veal			
das Kotelett	cutlet, chop		trinkbar	drinkable
das Mehl	flour		untrinkbar	undrinkable
das Mineralwasser	mineral water			
das Obst	fruit			

1 Put the words into the correct column.

Gemüse	Getränke	Obst

die Erbse   die Himbeere   der Kaffee   der Kakao   der Blumenkohl
die Kartoffel   die Apfelsine   der Kohl   der Orangensaft   die Pflaume
das Wasser   der Wein   die Weintraube   die Zitrone   die Zwiebel

2 Complete the star puzzles.

a A_____   A_____   P_____

H_____ ◄ *Obst* ► B_____

Z_____   E_____   B_____

b B_____   W_____   K_____

A_____ ◄ *Getränke* ► T_____

C_____   W_____   K_____

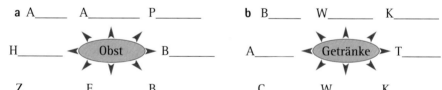
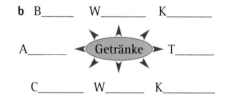

3 Complete the words by adding to the letters given. Give three words each time.

AP ► _ _ _ _ _ _
       _ _ _
       _ _ _ _ _ _

KA ► _ _ _ _ _ _ _ _
       _ _ _ _ _ _ _
       _ _ _ _

BR ► _ _
       _ _ _ _ _ _
       _ _ _ _ _ _ _

SCH ► _ _ _ _ _
        _ _ _ _ _ _ _
        _ _ _ _

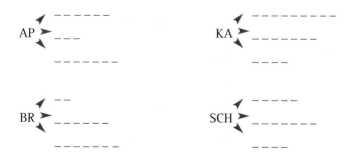

4 Give the genders of these words:

Kartoffel	Schinken	Birne	Reis	Kohl
Pfeffer	Salz	Obst	Käse	Wurst

5 Give German words for the following:

a two yellow fruits

b four types of sausage

c four flavours of ice-cream

d five types of meat

e four milk products

6 Complete these pairs.

a Brot mit _____

b Fisch mit _____

c Salz und _____

d Erdbeeren mit _____

e Milch und _____

7 Which food items are being described?

a Eine Obstsorte: rund, grün oder rot, gut für die Zähne.

b Eine Gemüsesorte: rund, klein und grün.

c Eine Obstsorte: gelb, schmeckt sauer.

d Eine Gemüsesorte: rund; außen braun, innen weiß; man weint, wenn man sie schneidet.

e Fleisch vom Schwein: rot, oft in Scheiben mit Eiern.

f Ein Getränk: heiß, mit Milch, Zucker oder Zitrone, Engländer trinken viel davon.

g Kartoffeln in dünnen Scheiben, in einer Packung.

8 What are these well known foods? Give the German word and its gender.

a Golden Delicious   b Nescafé   c Cheddar   d Boddington's

e Basmati   f Colman's   g Typhoo   h King Edward

der Becher	mug, cup, beaker
der Champignon	mushroom
der Durst	thirst
der Geruch	smell
der Geschmack	taste
der Hocker	stool
der Hunger	hunger
der Imbiss	snack*
der Kaffee	coffee
der Kellner	waiter
der Löffel	spoon
der Ofen	oven*
der Strohhalm	straw
der Teelöffel	teaspoon
der Teller	plate
der Tisch	table
der Topf	pan, dish

die Bar	bar
die Bedienung	service
die Bohne	bean
die Forelle	trout
die Gabel	fork
die Gaststätte	pub, restaurant
die Getränkekarte	wine list
die Imbisshalle	snackbar
die Kanne	pot
die Kneipe	pub
die Nachspeise	pudding
die Portion	portion
die Schale	bowl

die Selbstbedienung	self-service
die Serviette	serviette
die Speisekarte	menu
die Spezialität	speciality
die Suppe	soup
die Tasse	cup
die Tischdecke	tablecloth
die Traube	grape
die Untertasse	saucer*
die Vorspeise	starter

das Besteck	cutlery
das Bier	beer
das Eis	ice-cream
das Café	café
das Gasthaus	pub, restaurant
das Geschirr	crockery
das Getränk	drink
das Glas	glass
das Hauptgericht	main course
das Kännchen	pot
das Menü	set menu
das Messer	knife
das Restaurant	restaurant
das Stück	piece
das Tagesmenü	menu of the day
das Trinkgeld	tip
das Wiener Schnitzel	veal cutlet, cooked in bread crumbs
das Wirthaus	pub

die Bratkartoffeln	fried potatoes
die Meeresfrüchte	seafood

bedienen	to serve
bestellen	to order
bezahlen	to pay
braten	to fry
den Tisch decken	to set the table*
gern haben	to like
lieber haben	to prefer
probieren	to try
reichen	to pass
reservieren	to reserve
riechen	to smell
schmecken	to taste
sich zu Tisch setzen	to sit down at the table
servieren	to serve
zahlen	to pay

Das stimmt so	That's okay, keep the change
durstig	thirsty
Fräulein!	Waitress!
Guten Appetit!	Enjoy your meal!
Hat's geschmeckt?	Did you enjoy your meal?
Herr Ober!	Waiter!
hungrig	hungry
ich hätte gern ...	I would like ...

lecker	tasty
Mehrwertsteuer	value added tax (VAT)
satt	full, satisfied
sauer	sour
süß	sweet
Zahlen, bitte.	The bill, please.

1 Write down the words for these items.

2 Match up the words in these two groups and give the meaning of each word.

> Schweinebraten   Getränk   Kännchen   Kellner   Nachspeise
> schmecken   Vorspeise

> Bier   Eis   Fleisch   Kaffee   lecker   Suppe   Trinkgeld

3 Put these phrases into chronological order as you would use them in a restaurant.

a Herr Ober, zahlen bitte.

b Ja, ich bin satt.

c Ich nehme das Menü, bitte.

d Das stimmt so.

e Auf Wiedersehen.

f Guten Tag. Ein Tisch für zwei Personen, bitte.

g Darf ich die Speisekarte sehen?

h Hat's geschmeckt?

i Guten Appetit!

4 Complete the words by adding to the letters given. Give three words every time.

5 Put these words into the order in which they would occur in a restaurant.

a bestellen   b bezahlen   c Hauptgericht   d Nachspeise

e Speisekarte   f Trinkgeld   g Vorspeise

6 Write down the German for:

a three places to eat

b three containers for drinks

c three courses in a meal

7 Solve these anagrams.

a stepSreakie

b rerobenip

c Gräntek

d eisVespor

e Whatussir

der Abenteuerfilm	adventure film	der Walkman	walkman*
der Ball	ball*	der Werbespot	advert, commercial
der Basketball	basketball		
der Besuch	visit		
der Bildschirm	screen (TV)	die Angelrute	fishing rod
der Bösewicht	baddie*	die Blockflöte	recorder
der Bulle	cop*	die Disko / Disco	disco
der Comic	comic	die Figur	character (in play, book etc)*
der Dokumentarfilm	documentary film		
der Eintrittspreis	admission fee	die Fernsehsendung	TV programme
der Fotoapparat	camera	die Freizeit	free time*
der Fußball	football	die Galerie	gallery
der Gruselfilm	horror film	die Geige	violin
der Held	hero*	die Heldin	heroine*
der Horrorfilm	horror film	die Kamera	camera
der Kopfhörer	headphones*	die Kirmes	funfair*
der Krimi	crime film/book	die Lektüre	reading material
der Kummerkasten	agony column*		
der Liebesfilm	love film	die Mannschaft	team
der Nachtklub	night club	die Musik	music
der Popstar	pop star	die Popmusik	pop music
der Rollschuh	roller skate	die Reportage	TV / radio report*
der Roman	novel		
der Sänger	singer	die Sendung	broadcast
der Schauspieler	actor	die Satellitenschüssel	satellite dish
der Schurke	baddie*	die Serie	serie
der Sitz	seat	die Seifenoper	soap opera
der Spaß	fun	die Tagesschau	TV news
der Spieler	player*	die Talkshow	chat show
der Sport	sport	die Unterhaltung	entertainment*
der Streikende	striker*	die Vorstellung	performance
der Tanz	dance		
der Titel	title	die Wochenzeitung	weekly newspaper
der Trickfilm	cartoon		

die Zeitung	newspaper	angeln	to fish
		ausgehen	to go out
das Abonnement	subscription*	bergsteigen	to go mountaineering*
das Brettspiel	board game*		
das Freibad	open-air swimming pool	besuchen	to visit
		faulenzen	to laze about
das Hallenbad	indoor swimming pool	fernsehen	to watch TV
		fotografieren	to photograph
das Kabelfernsehen	cable television*	(sich) interessieren für	to be interested in
das Klavier	piano		
das Lied	song	lesen	to read
das Mikrofon	microphone*	musizieren	to make music
das Mitglied	member	Rad fahren	to cycle
das Programm	programme	reiten	to ride (horse)
das Ruderboot	rowing boat*	Rollschuh laufen	to rollerskate
das Satellitenbild	satellite picture	sammeln	to collect
		schwimmen	to swim
das Satellitenfernsehen	satellite TV	(im Chor) singen	to sing (in a choir)
das Schlagzeug	percussion	skateboarden	to skateboard
das Spiel	game*	spazieren gehen	to go for a walk
das Spielzeng	toy	spielen	to play
das Tournier	tournament*	tanzen	to dance
das Theaterstück	play	tauchen	to dive
		ein Tor schießen	to score a goal*
die Nachrichten	news*	trainieren	to train*
		treffen	to meet
Badminton	badminton	üben	practise
Fußball	football	wandern	to walk, hike*
Pop	pop		
Schach	chess	ausverkauft	sold out
Tennis	tennis	unentschieden	a draw (match)
Tischtennis	tabletennis		

1 What are these people doing? Write down the verbs.

2 Match up five pairs of words which go together from this list.

schwimmen	musizieren	lesen	treffen	das Hallenbad
die Lektüre	die Spieler	ausgehen	das Klavier	die Mannschaft

3 Write down:

  a two things to read

  b two indoor sports or games

  c five words to do with music

  d five words to do with the cinema

4 When you do these sports, how do you play? Write M for 'in einer Mannschaft', write P for 'mit einem Partner' and write A for 'allein'.

Angeln	Badminton	Fußball	Rad fahren	Reiten
Rollschuh laufen	Schach	Schwimmen	Tanzen	Tennis

5 Add extra parts to make longer words. Write down the meaning of the new words.

  a Theater   d Oper   g Bad

  b Tennis   e Schüssel   h Nacht

  c Ball   f Spieler

6 Complete the answers by writing down the correct verb.

| singen   sammeln   sehen   schwimmen   fotografieren |

> Remember the ending for 'ich': ....e.

a Magst du musizieren? Ja, ich _____ im Chor.

b Gehst du oft ins Kino? Ja, ich _____ gern Filme.

c Gehst du ins Hallenbad? Ja, ich _____ sehr gern.

d Hast du einen Fotoapparat? Ja, ich _____ meine Familie.

e Hast du ein Hobby? Ja, ich _____ Briefmarken.

7 Give the past participles for:

a schwimmen   **c** schießen   **e** lesen

b besuchen   **d** treffen

Now write the correct words in these sentences:

a Ich habe meine Oma _____.

b Ich habe im Hallenbad _____.

c Ich habe die Zeitung _____.

d Ich habe meine Freunde _____.

e Vor dem Konzert hat das Orchester viel _____.

8 Where do these words belong? Write L for 'lesen', M for 'Musik' and K for 'Kino'.

| die Lektüre   der Eintrittspreis   der Gruselfilm   das Klavier
die Wochenzeitung   die Geige   der Krimi   das Lied
der Roman   der Sänger   der Schauspieler
die Vorstellung   der Walkman |

der Ausdruck	expression
der Charakter	character
der Komponist	composer*
der Mensch	person, human being
der Pferdeschwanz	ponytail*
der Pony	fringe*
der Streit	argument, quarrel

die Angst	fear
die Freude	joy
die Laune	mood*
die Liebe	love
die Nerven	nerves
die Persönlichkeit	personality

das Gelaber	waffle*
das Verhältnis	relationship
das Vertrauen	trust

besprechen	to discuss
bevorzugen	to prefer
erwachsen	to arise, develop, grow
gefallen	to please
labern	to waffle
lachen	to laugh
lächeln	to smile
lügen	to lie
Recht haben	to be right*

in schlechter Laune sein	to be in a bad mood*
schreien	to cry, shout
schwärmen für	to be crazy about
Unrecht haben	to be wrong*
(sich) verstehen	to get on with someone
verliebt sein	to be in love
weinen	to cry

allein	alone
arm	poor
attraktiv	attractive
behindert	disabled*
berühmt	famous
böse	angry
brav	well-behaved*
doof	stupid
dumm	stupid
ehrlich	honest
ernst	serious
faul	lazy
fleißig	hard-working
frech	cheeky
freundlich	friendly
geschwätzig/ gesprächig	chatty*
glücklich	happy
gut	good
höflich	polite
humorlos	humourless

intelligent	intelligent	streng	strict
interessant	interesting	sympathisch	pleasant
komisch	funny	traurig	sad
klug	clever	treu	loyal
launisch	moody	typisch	typical
laut	loud	unartig	naughty
leise	quiet	unehrlich	dishonest
lieb	nice, kind	unfreundlich	unfriendly
lockig	curly	ungeduldig	impatient
lustig	funny	unglücklich	unhappy
nett	nice	unhöflich	impolite
optimistisch	optimistic	unzufrieden	discontented
pessimistisch	pessimistic	verantwortlich	responsible
praktisch	practical	vergesslich	absent-minded*
pünktlich	prompt	vorsichtig	careful
reich	rich	witzig	funny
ruhig	quiet	zufrieden	content
schüchtern	shy	zuverlässig	reliable*
selbstsüchtig	selfish		

1 What adjectives describe these people?

2 Are these adjectives positive (+) or negative (-)?

a doof		**e** faul	
b launisch		**f** ungeduldig	
c nett		**g** freundlich	
d unhöflich		**h** brav	

3 Write down:

  a three words ending in 'n'

  b four words ending in 'lich'

  c nine words ending in 'ig'

4 Write the opposites of these words.

  a dumm

  b laut

  c glücklich

  d faul

  e höflich

  f reich

  g geduldig

  h schwätzig

5 Write an adjective describing someone's personality for each letter of the alphabet.

  (There are no words for the letters C, J, M, Q, X, Y.)

6 Use an adjective to fill the gaps in these sentences.

  a Er war sehr _____. Sein Gesicht war rot.

  b Er bleibt bis elf Uhr im Bett. Er ist sehr _____.

  c Er spricht nicht viel. Er ist sehr _____.

  d Die Familie ist _____: Sie hat nicht viel Geld.

  e Sylvester Stallone ist ein _____ Schauspieler.

  f Er lacht nicht viel. Er ist sehr _____.

  g Diese Frauen plaudern oft. Sie sind sehr _____.

  h Er lügt nie. Er ist sehr _____.

der Abend	evening	(sich) kennen lernen	to get to know (each other)
der Augenblick	moment	(sich) setzen	to sit down
der Moment	moment	siezen	to call someone 'Sie'
der Monat	month		
der Morgen	morning	einen Termin machen	to make an appointment
der Nachmittag	afternoon		
der Punkt	point, dot	treffen	to meet
der Tag	day	(sich) verabschieden	to take one's leave
der Termin	date, deadline		
der Vormittag	morning	(sich) vorstellen	to introduce oneself
die Minute	minute	willkommen heißen	to welcome
die Sekunde	second		
die Uhr	hour	abgemacht	agreed
die Woche	week	auf Wiederhören	goodbye (on phone)
die Zeit	time		
		auf Wiedersehen	goodbye
das Handy	mobile phone	danke (schön)	thank you (very much)
das Datum	date		
das Jahr	year	Grüß Gott	hello (Bavarian)
das Mal	time, occasion		
das Wochenende	weekend	Hallo	hello
		herzlich willkommen	welcome
begrüßen	to greet		
duzen	to call someone 'du'	hoffentlich	I hope that
		Lust haben	to want
empfangen	to receive, greet, welcome	Servus	hello, goodbye (S. Germany)
(sich) freuen	to be pleased	um halb sieben	at half past six
(sich) freuen auf	to look forward to	um sechs Uhr	at six o'clock
hoffen	to hope	um Viertel nach sechs	at a quarter past six
kennen	to know	Wie geht's?	How are you?

Montag	Monday	täglich	daily
Dienstag	Tuesday	übermorgen	day after tomorrow
Mittwoch	Wednesday		
Donnerstag	Thursday	vorgestern	day before yesterday
Freitag	Friday		
Samstag	Saturday		
Sonnabend	Saturday (N. Germany)	Januar	January
		Februar	February
Sonntag	Sunday	März	March
		April	April
montags, usw.	on Mondays, etc.	Mai	May
		Juni	June
bis	until	Juli	July
gestern	yesterday	August	August
heute	today	September	September
heute Abend	this evening	Oktober	October
heute Morgen	this morning	November	November
heute Nachmittag	this afternoon	Dezember	December
jede	every		
jetzt	now	Der wievielte ist heute?	What's the date today?
letzte	last		
manchmal	sometimes	Treffen wir uns um...	Let's meet at...
Mittag	midday		
Mitternacht	midnight	Wie spät ist es?	What time is it?
morgen	tomorrow		
morgen früh	tomorrow morning	Wie viel Uhr ist es?	What time is it?
nachher	afterwards		
nächste	next		
nun	now		
sofort	immediately		

1 Put these phrases into chronological order. Start with the one furthest in the past.

übermorgen   gestern   nächste Woche   letzte Woche
nächstes Jahr   morgen   vorgestern   heute

2 Write down the day and date in words:

a Sa. 11.1

b Mi. 22.3

c Do. 19.5

d So. 8.12

e Fr. 30.11

f Di. 15.10

g Mo. 14.7

h Do. 12.8

3 Answer these vocabulary sums.

a   eine Sekunde x 60 =

b   ein Monat x 12 =

c   ein Tag x 7 =

d   eine Stunde x 24 =

e   Samstag + Sonntag =

f   eine Woche x 4 =

4 Coming or going? When would you say these phrases? Write A for when you arrive and L for when you leave.

a Guten Morgen.

b Bis morgen, also.

c Herzlich willkommen.

d Auf Wiedersehen.

e Es freut mich, Sie kennenzulernen.

f Schönes Wochenende.

g Wie geht's?

h Grüß Gott.

5 Write two different ways of saying the following in German:

a Saturday

b morning

c six thirty

d now

e every day

6 Solve these word puzzles.

   a ein Tag mit ‚schlechtem Wetter‘

   b ein Tag ohne ‚Tag‘

   c ein Tag, wo man immer ‚Sonne‘ hat

   d Ist alles ‚kostenlos‘ an diesem Tag?

7 Solve these anagrams. Each word starts with the letter in the middle.

a

a	c	h
a	**m**	n
m	l	

b

n	t	h	f
	f	**h**	c
l	o	i	e

c

	r	e
m	**T**	n
	i	

d

h	i	g	m
	t	**N**	a
a	t	c	

e

a	e	o
d	**S**	n
n	b	n

8 Add another part to make a longer word. Give the meaning of both words.

   a Abend

   b kommen

   c Mittag

   d morgen

   e gestern

   f Woche

9 Solve these dingbats.

   a gen
      mor

   b mittag der

   c w o c h e n e n d e

der Ausverkauf	sale		die Eisenwaren-	
der Cent	cent		handlung	hardware shop*
der Euro	euro (money)		die Etage	floor
der Feiertag	public holiday		die Flasche	bottle
der Fischhändler	fishmonger		die Fleischerei	butchers
der Franken	franc		die Geschäftszeit	opening hours
	(Switzerland)		die Kasse	cash desk
der Groschen	groschen		die Konditorei	cake shop
der Korb	basket		die Kreditkarte	credit card
der Kunde	customer		die Liste	list
der Laden	shop		die Mark	mark (money)
der Ladenbesitzer	shopkeeper*		die Metzgerei	butchers
der Liter	liter		die Packung	packet
der Markt	market		die Quittung	receipt
der Preis	price		die Rolltreppe	escalator*
der Scheck	cheque		die Schachtel	box
der Schein	bank note		die Scheibe	slice
der Schilling	schilling		die	
	(Austria)		Selbstbedienung	self-service*
der Stock	floor		die Tasche	shopping bag
der Supermarkt	supermarket		die Tube	tube
der Verkäufer	salesperson		die Tüte	bag
der Zehnmarkschein	ten-mark note		die Verkäuferin	salesperson
der Zeitungskiosk	newspaper			(female)
	kiosk			

die Abteilung	department		das Andenken	souvenir
die Apotheke	chemist		das Angebot	offer
die Auswahl	choice*		das Bargeld	cash
die Bäckerei	bakery		das Bonbon	sweet
die Brieftasche	wallet		das Dutzend	dozen
die Buchhandlung	bookshop		das Erdgeschoss	ground floor
die Dose	tin		das Fenster	window
die Drogerie	chemist*		das Geschäft	shop
die Einkaufsliste	shopping list		das Gramm	gram
			das Kaufhaus	department
				store*

das Kilo	kilo	kaufen	to buy
das Lebensmittel-		kosten	to cost
geschäft	grocer's	öffnen	to open
das Päckchen	packet*	die Quittung	to keep the
das Paket	packet*	behalten	receipt*
das Portemonnaie	purse	schließen	to close
das Pfund	pound (weight,	verkaufen	to sell
	English	wert sein	to be worth*
	money)		
das Regal	shelf	ausverkauft	sold out
das Schaufenster	display window	billig	cheap
das Schreibwaren-		ein bisschen	a bit
geschäft	stationer's	ein paar	a few
das Sonderangebot	special offer	ein wenig	a little
das Stück	piece	einige	some
das		einschließlich	inclusive,
Süßwarengeschäft	sweet shop		including
das Untergeschoss	basement*	genug	enough
das Warenhaus	department	geöffnet	open
	store	geschlossen	closed
das Zentimeter	centimetre	gratis	free
		kostenlos	free
die Einkäufe	purchases	offen	open
die Lebensmittel	groceries	preiswert	value for
die Öffnungszeiten	opening hours*		money
die Tabakwaren	tobacco goods	pro	each
		reduziert	reduced
ausgeben	to spend	sehen Sie sich	browsers
sich beschweren	to complain*	unverbindlich um	welcome*
bezahlen	to pay (for)	teuer	expensive
Einkäufe machen	to do some	wie viel	how much
	shopping	wie viele	how many
einkaufen gehen	to go shopping	zu verkaufen	for sale
einwickeln	to wrap*		
geben	to give		
das Geld	to be		
zurückbekommen	reimbursed*		

1 Write down the names of these items.

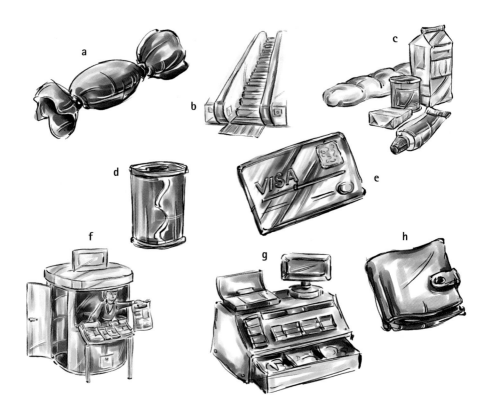

2 What are these items? Write **C** for currency, **W** for weight or **M** for a measure. Watch out! One of the words has two answers!

a Gramm **b** Liter **c** Franken **d** Euro **e** Pfund
f Groschen **g** Kilo

3 In which shop would you buy these items?

a das Brot **b** das Schreibpapier **c** das Buch **d** der Kuchen
e das Fleisch **f** die Butter **g** die Tabletten

4 Fill in the gaps in this text.

Ich bin in den Supermarkt gegangen. Das Geschäft ist von 9 Uhr bis 7 Uhr
a _____, und heute haben sie viele _____. Ich gehe gern in
dieses Geschäft: Die **c** _____ ist immer groß. Ich habe eine
d _____ Milch, eine **e** _____ Suppe und ein **f** _____ Eier gekauft.
Ich konnte keine Chips kaufen: Das **g** _____ war leer. In der
Gemüse **h**_____ habe ich ein **i** _____ Kartoffeln gekauft. Ich
habe an der **j** _____ bezahlt. Die Kassiererin hat mir die
k _____ gegeben. Alles hat nur €3 gekostet. Ich finde, das ist sehr
l _____. Ich habe alles in meine **m** _____ getan und dann bin
ich nach Hause gegangen.

5 Add to these words to form a longer word. Write down the meaning of both words.

a Tasche   **b** Markt   **c** Karte   **d** Liste   **e** kaufen   **f** Fenster
g Zeit   **h** Haus   **i** Geld   **j** geben

6 Make ten words from these parts of words. Each word has three parts.

ab	aus	buch	ein	fen	ge	ger	geschäft	hand	kaufs
kauft	kosten	lebens	los	lung	metz	mittel	ei	schau
schoss	ster	teil	ung	unter	ver	liste

7 Write down:

a the names of five shops

b three ways of making a payment

c four containers

d three weights

der Gürtel	belt		die Hose	trousers
der Handschuh	glove		die Jacke	jacket
der Hut	hat		die Jeans	jeans
der Knopf	button		die Kette	chain, necklace
der Lippenstift	lipstick		die Kleidung	clothing
der Mantel	coat		die Krawatte	tie
der Modezeichner	fashion designer		die kurze Hose	shorts
			die Marke	brand, make*
der Nagellack	nail varnish*		die Mode	fashion
der Pulli	pullover		die Modezeitschrift	fashion magazine*
der Pullover	pullover			
der Regenmantel	raincoat		die Mütze	cap
der Regenschirm	umbrella		die Sandale	sandal
der Reißverschluss	zip*		die Schminke	make-up
der Ring	ring		die Seide	silk*
der Rock	skirt		die Shorts	shorts
der Sakko	sports jacket		die Socke	sock
der Schal	scarf		die Werbeagentur	advertising agency
der Schlafanzug	pyjamas			
der Schlips	tie		die Wolle	wool
der Schmuck	jewellery			
der Schuh	shoe		das Hemd	shirt
der Stiefel	boot		das Kleid	dress
der Teint	complexion*		das Leder	leather
			das Make-up	make-up
die Armbanduhr	wristwatch		das Paar	pair*
die Baumwolle	cotton		das Parfüm	perfume
die Badehose	swimming trunks		das Sweatshirt	sweatshirt
			das Taschentuch	handkerchief
die Bluse	blouse		das T-Shirt	t-shirt
die Farbe	colour			
die Größe	size			

die Klamotten	clothes (slang)	eingelaufen	shrunk*
die Lippen	lips	gelb	yellow
die Ohrringe	earrings	gold	gold
		grau	grey
anprobieren	to try on	grün	green
anziehen	to put on	hell	light
ausziehen	to take off	lila	lilac
passen	to fit, to suit	modern	modern
sich schminken	to put on make-up	modisch	fashionable
		orange	orange
stehen	to suit	rein	pure
tragen	to wear	rosa	pink
umtauschen	to exchange	rot	red
(sich) umziehen	to change	schick	chic, fashionable
vergleichen	to compare		
vorziehen	to prefer	schwarz	black
		wasserdicht	waterproof
bequem	comfortable	wasserfest	waterproof
blau	blue	weiß	white
braun	brown		
bunt	bright, colourful	Welche Größe haben Sie?	What size do you take?
dunkel	dark		
echt	genuine		

1 Write down the names of these items of clothing.

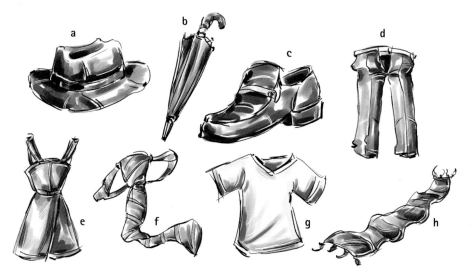

2 Add another part to each word to make a new word. Write down the meaning of both words.

a Arm   b Mantel   c Wolle   d Lippen   e Hose
f Schuh   g Ring

3 Write down:

a two words for 'tie'

b three colours beginning with 'g'

c four items where the English word is the same as the German word

d four verbs ending in 'ziehen'

4 What clothes would you wear on these parts of the body?

a die Hand   b der Kopf   c das Ohr   d der Hals
e der Fuß   f die Beine

5 **Fill in the missing words in these sentences.**

a Kann ich bitte diese Jacke _____?

b Welche _____ haben Sie?

c Ich möchte schwimmen, aber ich habe meine _____ vergessen.

d Es regnet. Nimm deinen _____ und deinen _____ mit.

e Das Kleid ist jetzt zu klein. Es ist _____.

f Die Schuhe sind nicht _____. Sie sind zu klein.

g Ich kann diese Hose nicht mehr tragen. Der _____ ist kaputt.

6 **Complete the words by adding to the given letter(s). Give three words every time.**

7 **Write down the colour(s) of the following:**

a das Gras
b eine Zitrone
c ein Elefant
d die Ampel (drei)
e das Trikot von Manchester United
f ein Ei (zwei)
g die britische Flagge (drei)
h Erdbeereis
i die österreichische Flagge
j Sahne

der Abfall	rubbish, waste	die Obdachlosigkeit	homelessness
der Alkohol	alcohol	die Ozonschicht	ozone layer*
der Aussiedler	emigrant*	die Politik	politics*
der Delphin	dolphin*	die Überschwemmung	flood
der Dieb	thief*	die Umwelt	environment
der Diebstahl	theft*	die Umwelt- verschmutzung	environmental pollution
der Drogensüchtige	drug addict*	die Welt	world
der Einsturz	collapse (of a building)*	die Wiederverwertung	recycling*
der Einwanderer	immigrant*		
der Flüchtling	refugee*		
der Haushaltsmüll	household refuse*	das Aids	Aids*
der Ladendiebstahl	shoplifting*	das Erdbeben	earthquake*
der Lärm	noise	das Kernkraftwerk	nuclear power station*
der Müll	rubbish		
der Obdachlose	homeless person*	die entwickelten Länder	developed countries*
der Ölteppich	oil slick*	die Entwicklungsländer	developing countries*
der Regenwald	rainforest*		
der Treibhausaffekt	greenhouse effect*	aufschlagen	to open up
der Vandalismus	vandalism*	ausgeben	to spend
		bekämpfen	to fight, combat*
die Arbeitslosigkeit	unemployment	sparen	to save
die Brutalität	brutality	verschmutzen	to pollute*
die Chemikalie	chemical*	verstehen	to understand
die Dritte Welt	third world*	Zuflucht suchen	to take refuge*
die Droge	drug		
die Dürre	drought*	obdachlos	homeless*
die Ebbe	low tide*	sauber	clean
die Flasche	bottle	schmutzig	dirty
die Gesellschaft	society*		
die Gewalt	violence*		
die Luft	air		
die Mehrwegflasche	returnable bottle		

1 What social issues are being described in these sentences?

a Man hat alle Fenster in der Schule kaputtgeschlagen.

b Man 'geht einkaufen' ohne Geld.

c Zu viele junge Leute werden betrunken.

d Papier, leere Flaschen, Dosen, usw. liegen auf der Straße.

e Wir bringen unsere Flaschen und Dosen immer zum Container.

f Es gibt zu viele Autos auf unseren Straßen.

g Viele Leute haben kein Haus: Sie schlafen auf der Straße.

h Viele junge Leute bekommen heute keine Stelle.

i Musik, Autos, Flugzeuge, es ist alles so laut.

2 Add another part to each word to make a longer word. Write down the meaning of both words.

a Laden   b Haus   c Umwelt   d Ozon   e wieder   f geben

3 Fill in the missing words in these sentences.

a Die Luft ist heute so _____.

b Mach das Licht aus! Wir müssen Energie _____.

c Viele _____ sind von Afrika nach Deutschland gekommen.

d _____ ist ungesund. Du solltest es aufgeben.

e Er schläft auf einer Bank im Park. Er ist _____.

f Zu viele Leute kaufen Cola in Dosen. Sie sollten _____ kaufen.

4 Find eight words in this 'chain'. Write down their meanings.

idasauberiotndiebohebbeotaweltämlufteraregenwaldootergewaltumlärm

der Bauer	farmer*	die Büroklammer	paper clip*
der Besitzer	owner*	die CD-ROM	CD-ROM*
der Einbrecher	burglar*	die E-Mail	e-mail*
der Eindruck	impression	die Datei	file (computer)*
der Frühling	spring	die Datenbank	database*
der Gewerkschaftler	trade unionist*	die Debatte	debate*
der Gott	god	die Dokumentation	documentation
der Grund	reason	die Erde	earth*
der Hausmeister	caretaker*	die Erlaubnis	permission*
der Herbst	autumn	die Festplatte	hard disk*
der Kampf	battle*	die Homepage	homepage
der Kleber	glue stick*	die Meinung	opinion
der Klebstoff	glue*	die Patrone	ink cartridge (for pen)*
der Kommentar	commentary (statement of personal opinion)*	die Sprache	language
		die Tastatur	keyboard
		die Taste	key (on keyboard)
der Korrekturstift	tippex pen*	die Tinte	ink*
der Locher	hole punch*	die Webpage / Webseite	web page
der Mikrochip	microchip*		
der Plan	plan	die Weinernte	grape harvest*
der Rauch	smoke*	die Weinlese	grape harvest*
der Rechner	calculator		
der Schläger	thug*	das Beispiel	example
der Sommer	summer	das CD-ROM-Laufwerk	CD-ROM drive*
der Stern	star	das Diskettenlaufwerk	floppy disk drive*
der Stift	pen	das Holz	wood
der Tageslichtprojektor	OHP*	das Meter	metre
der Teil	part	das Passwort	password*
der Tesafilm	sellotape*	das Plastik	plastic
der Tippfehler	typing error	das Polizeirevier	policestation
der Wettbewerb	competition*	das Viertel	quarter
der Winter	winter		
die Art	kind, sort		
die Ausstellung	exhibition		

die Ziffern	figures	Leid tun (Es tut mir Leid.)	to be sorry (I'm sorry.)
		liegen	to lie, be situated
abholen	to fetch		
abladen	to download*	machen	to make, do
abschleppen	to drag, haul off, tow away	meinen	to think, have an opinion
abschreiben	to copy*	messen	to measure
ansehen	to look at (closely)	müssen	to have to, must
aufmachen	to open	raten	to guess, advise
ausdrücken	to express	rechnen	to calculate
aussprechen	to pronounce	rennen	to run, race
bearbeiten	to work on, deal with, edit	retten	to save
		sagen	to say
begleiten	to accompany	schützen	to protect
bekommen	to get	sehen	to see
brauchen	to need	sein	to be
denken (an)	to think (of)	sitzen	to sit
drehen	to turn	sollen	to ought to, should
dürfen	to be allowed		
eingießen	to pour in	sprechen	to speak
erlauben	to allow	stehen	to stand
erzählen	to tell (story)	sterben	to die
formatieren	to format*	töten	to kill*
geben	to give	verbringen	to spend time
gebrauchen	to use	vergessen	to forget
gehören	to belong	verlieren	to lose
glauben	to believe, think	versuchen	to try
haben	to have	weitermachen	to continue
halten	to stop	wiederholen	to repeat
hängen	to hang	wissen	to know
holen	to fetch	wollen	to want
kämpfen	to fight	wünschen	to wish
können	to be able	zeigen	to show
laden	to load*	ziehen	to pull
laufen	to run	zu den Akten legen	to file

beschäftigt	busy	als	as, when
besser	better	also	therefore
breit	broad, wide	am besten	best
eng	narrow	am liebsten	best
enttäuschend	disappointing	auch	also
enttäuscht	disappointed	bald	soon
erlaubt	allowed*	beide	both
falsch	wrong	besonders	especially
frisch	fresh	(ein) bisschen	(a) bit
glatt	smooth	bitte	please
hart	hard	bleiben Sie bitte	hold the line
hoch	high	am Apparat	
kaputt	broken	d.h. (das heißt)	i.e. (that is)
langsam	slow	da	there, as
leer	empty	damals	then
müde	tired	damit	so that
neu	new	dann	then
nötig	necessary	dass	that
nützlich	useful	dieser	this
richtig	right, correct	diesmal	this time
schlecht	bad	doch	but yes
schlimm	bad	dort	there
schnell	quick, fast	endlich	at last
schrecklich	dreadful*	es gefällt mir	I like it
schriftlich	in writing	es geht	it's OK
schwierig	difficult	es gibt	there is
sportlich	sporting	etwa	about
still	quiet	etwas	something
toll	great	fast	almost
voll	full	genau	exactly
wichtig	important	gerade	just, straight
wunderbar	wonderful	gewöhnlich	usually
		halb	half
		heutzutage	nowadays
aber	but	hier	here
alles	everything		

immer	always	sogar	even
immer noch	still	sonst	otherwise
in Ordnung	in order	überall	everywhere
im Voraus	in advance	unbedingt	absolutely
jemand	someone	unmöglich	impossible
leider	unfortunately	unterwegs	on the way
Lieblings...	favourite ...	usw.	etc.
man	one, 'they'	Verzeihung!	Sorry!
mehr	more	vielleicht	perhaps
mehrere	several	völlig	completely
möglich	possible	vor	in front of
natürlich	naturally, of course	vorher	previously
		wahrscheinlich	probably
neben	next to	wann	when
neulich	recently	warum	why
nicht mehr	no longer	was	what
nichts	nothing	was für	what kind of
nie	never	weil	because
niemand	no-one	wenig	few
noch einmal	again	wenn	whenever, if
noch nicht	not yet	wer	who
normalerweise	usually	wie	how
nur	only	Wie, bitte?	Pardon?
ob	whether	wieder	again
oder	or	wirklich	really
plötzlich	suddenly	woher	where from
prima	great	wohin	where to
privat	private*	z.B. (zum Beispiel)	e.g. (for example)
schon	already		
selbst	even, self	ziemlich	rather
selten	rarely	zu Ende	over
sicher	safe, sure, certainly	zurück	back
		zusammen	together
so	thus		
so dass	so that		

If you can learn these simple rules they will help you form the plurals of most of the German nouns that you will meet in an examination.

1 Masculine nouns add Umlaut + 'e'

e.g. der Fuß   die Füße   der Kopf   die Köpfe

If no Umlaut is possible, just add 'e'

e.g. der Tisch   die Tische   der Brief   die Briefe

Exceptions

der Arm   die Arme   der Besuch   die Besuche

der Hund   die Hunde   der Monat   die Monate

der Schuh   die Schuhe   der Tag   die Tage

and

der Mann   die Männer   der Wald   die Wälder

2 Feminine nouns add 'n' or 'en'

e.g. die Frau   die Frauen   die Tasche   die Taschen

Some feminine nouns add Umlaut + 'e'

e.g. die Bank   die Bänke   die Hand   die Hände

die Kuh   die Kühe   die Maus   die Mäuse

die Nacht   die Nächte   die Stadt   die Städte

die Wand   die Wände   die Wurst   die Würste

Exceptions

die Mutter   die Mütter   die Tochter   die Töchter

3 Neuter nouns add Umlaut + 'er'

e.g. das Buch   die Bücher   das Glas   die Gläser

If no Umlaut is possible, just add 'e'

e.g. das Heft   die Hefte   das Pferd   die Pferde

Exceptions

das Bild	die Bilder	das Ei	die Eier
das Jahr	die Jahre	das Kind	die Kinder

4 Masculine and neuter nouns ending in -el, -er, -chen and -lein DON'T CHANGE.

e.g. der Füller   die Füller   das Fenster   die Fenster

der Schlüssel   die Schlüssel   das Mädchen   die Mädchen

Exceptions

der Garten	die Gärten	der Mantel	die Mäntel
der Vogel	die Vögel	der Vater	die Väter
der Bruder	die Brüder	der Apfel	die Äpfel
der Laden	die Läden		

5 'Weak' masculine nouns add 'n' or 'en'

e.g. der Herr   die Herren   der Junge   die Jungen

der Mensch   die Menschen   der Polizist   die Polizisten

der Student   die Studenten

6 Foreign neuters add 's'

e.g. das Auto   die Autos   das Baby   die Babys

das Kino   die Kinos

7 These five neuter nouns add 'n' or 'en'

das Auge	die Augen	das Bett	die Betten
das Ende	die Enden	das Hemd	die Hemden
das Ohr	die Ohren		

Activities

Write down the plurals of these nouns. Try applying the rules to other words that you have learned in this book.

das Haus	der Sohn	der Mann
die Blume	die Zeitung	der Füller
der Junge	der Stern	das Kaninchen
der Apfel	der Bleistift	das Passwort
der Kugelschreiber	die Gabel	das Buch
der Tisch	der Hund	der Brief
die Briefmarke	das Lineal	die Banane
die Taste	das Fenster	die Tür
die Schule	der Vater	das Heft
die Wand	die Lampe	das Hemd
der Polizist	der Vorhang	der Wegweiser
das Mädchen	das Blatt	der Bruder
der Rechner	der Schuh	die Autobahn
die Uhr	die Krawatte	das Bild
das Bad	die Hand	der Finger
der Arm	das Bein	der Kopf
das Geschenk	der Schrank	die Chemiekalie
die Mutter	das Bonbon	der Schläger
der Fuß	der Platz	

P r e p o s i t i o n s

Prepositions are very important in German, because the words which follow them have to change.

You say *mit <u>dem</u> Auto*, but *mit <u>der</u> U-Bahn*;

You say *für <u>meinen</u> Bruder*, but *für <u>meine</u> Schwester*.

It sounds very complicated, but it isn't really. Here are some rules to help you.

1 aus, außer, bei, mit, nach, seit, von, zu, gegenüber

aus	*out of*	seit	*since*
außer	*apart from, besides*	von	*from, of*
bei	*at (the house of)*	zu	*to*
mit	*with*	gegenüber	*opposite*
nach	*after*		

These prepositions are always followed by a word ending in 'm', 'r' or 'm'.

Just check the gender of the noun: is it *der, die* or *das*? Then remember:

	der	die	das
	⇩	⇩	⇩
	m	r	m
e.g.	dem	der	dem
	meinem	meiner	meinem

Examples

der Wagen ⇨ mit dem Wagen

die Schule ⇨ nach der Schule

das Fenster ⇨ aus dem Fenster

Try and write these in German:

a with my brother _____

b after the film _____

c at my sister's _____

d the girl's bike (the bike of the girl) _____

Did you get them right? You do them like this:

a *mit* + *der Bruder*, so the word following *mit* ends with 'm': *mit dem Bruder*

b *nach* + *der* Film, so the word following *nach* ends with 'm': *nach dem Film*

c *bei* + *die Schwester*, so the word following *bei* ends with 'r': *bei der Schwester*

d *von* + *das Mädchen*, so the word following *von* ends with 'm': *das Fahrrad von dem Mädchen.*

Now try exercise 1 on page 97.

2 durch, für, entlang, gegen, ohne, um

durch	*through*	gegen	*against, towards*
für	*for*	ohne	*without*
entlang	*along*	um	*around*

These prepositions are always followed by *den, die* or *das,* or *einen, eine* or *ein.**

(*Notice there is no 's' here.)

So again, just check the gender of the noun: is it *der, die* or *das*? Then remember:

	der	**die**	**das**	
	⇩	⇩	⇩	
	n	e	s	(but NO 's' with *ein, mein,* etc.)
e.g.	den	die	das	
	einen	eine	ein	

Examples

der Bruder ⇨ für meinen Bruder

die Stadt ⇨ um die Stadt

das Wasser ⇨ durch das Wasser

Try and write these in German:

a for my brother _____

c through the window _____

b without his jacket _____

d for a year _____

These work out like this:

a *für* + *der Bruder*, so the word following *für* ends with 'n': *für den Bruder*

b *ohne* + *die Jacke*, so the word following *ohne* ends with 'e': *ohne die Jacke*

c *durch* + *das Fenster*, so the word following *durch* ends with 's': *durch das Fenster*

d *für* + *das Jahr*. The word following *für* normally ends with 's', but we are using *ein*, which cannot end with 's', so it's: *für ein Jahr*.

Now try exercise 2 on page 97.

3 an, auf, hinter, in, neben, über, unter, vor, zwischen

an	*on (a vertical surface)*	über	*over, above*
auf	*on (a horizontal surface)*	unter	*under*
hinter	*behind*	vor	*in front of (outside)*
in	*in*	zwischen	*between*
neben	*next to*		

These prepositions work in two ways:

A If they are saying **where** something is, they work like group 1,

e.g. The book is on the table.   *Das Buch ist* **auf dem** *Tisch.*

The garage is behind the house. *Die Garage ist* **hinter dem** *Haus.*

B If they indicate **movement towards** the thing being spoken about, they work like group 2,

e.g. I drive the car into the garage.	*Ich fahre das Auto* in die Garage.
I am going to the cinema.	*Ich gehe* ins *(in das)* Kino.

Which group do these sentences belong to?

a The cat is under the table.

b I put it into my pocket.

c The library is next to the town hall.

d I am going into town.

e I'll meet you outside the cinema.

Did you get them right?

a Group 1   **b** Group 2   **c** Group 1   **d** Group 2   **e** Group 1

Now try to put the sentences into German.

a Die Katze ist unter dem Tisch.

b Ich stecke es in meine Tasche.

c Die Bibliothek ist neben dem Rathaus.

d Ich fahre in die Stadt.

e Ich treffe dich vor dem Kino.

Now try exercise 3 on page 98.

When you can get the singular right almost every time, ask your teacher to explain the plural to you.

4 Plurals

In the plural, you do not have to worry about the gender of the noun.

A The words in **Group 1** are simply followed by a word ending in 'n', e.g. *mit meinen Schwestern.*

Notice also that you put an 'n' on the end of the noun if it does not already have one, e.g. *mit den Fahrrädern.*

Look at the section on plurals (page 90) to help you with plural forms.

B The words in **Group** 2 are followed by a word ending in 'e', e.g. *für meine Eltern.*

C The words in **Group 3** still work in the same way:

Like Group 1 when there is no movement, e.g. *Die Garagen sind hinter* den Häusern.

Like Group 2 for **movement towards** the object, e.g. *Wir fahren die Autos in* die Garagen.

Activities

1

a Ich fahre mit _____ Straßenbahn.

b Nach _____ Abendessen mache ich die Hausaufgaben.

c Ich wohne seit _____ Jahr in Hamburg.

d Ich verbringe den Sommer bei _____ Tante in Berlin.

e Das ist ein Geschenk von _____ Oma.

f Das Rathaus ist gegenüber _____ Bahnhof.

g Ich gehe zu Fuß _____ Schule.

h Er ist ein Freund von _____ Schwester.

i Ich fahre sehr oft mit _____ Rad.

j Fahren Sie _____ Stadion?

2

a Diese Blumen sind für _____ Mutter.

b Gehen Sie hier _____ Straße entlang.

c Das kannst du ohne _____ Hilfe machen.

d Um _____ Dom herum gibt es viele schöne Geschäfte.

e Vielen Dank für _____ Brief.

f Die Familie sitzt um _____ Tisch.

g Ich habe es für _____ Bruder gekauft.

h Ohne _____ Partner kann ich nicht Tennis spielen.

i Wir machen einen Spaziergang ____ Fluß entlang.

j Er warf den Ball durch ____ Fenster.

3

a In _____ Schlafzimmer gibt es ein Bett.

b Meine Schuhe sind unter ____ Bett.

c Der Tisch ist in ___ Mitte des Zimmers.

d Ich habe viele Poster an _____ Wand.

e Der Stuhl ist neben _____ Tisch.

f Ich hänge meine Kleider in _____ Schrank.

g Meine Jacke hängt hinter _____ Tür.

h Um zehn Uhr gehe ich in ____ Bett.

i Mein Bruder darf nicht in _____ Zimmer kommen.

j Das Badezimmer ist neben _____ Schlafzimmer.

4

This exercise combines all the prepositions. See how much you have learned!

a Ich gehe mit _____ Mutter einkaufen.

b In _____ Fußgängerzone kann man sehr gut einkaufen.

c Nach _____ Schule mache ich die Hausaufgaben.

d Mit _____ Taschengeld kaufe ich Bonbons und CDs.

e Der Bleistift? Er liegt auf _____ Tisch.

f Kannst du das alles in _____ Küche bringen?

g Das Auto ist in _____ Garage.

h Ich fahre mit _____ Bus _____ Schule.

i Ich bin mit _____ Freund in _____ Kino gegangen.

j Wir treffen uns vor ____ Bahnhof und dann gehen wir in ____ Café.

For the reading and listening tests it is very important that you learn the question words well. Many candidates give the wrong answer because they do not read the question words carefully enough.

wer	*who*
was	*what*
wo	*where*
warum	*why*
wann	*when*

Wer works like *der.* So:

für wen	*for whom (who for)*
mit wem	*with whom (who with)*
bei wem	*at whose house*
von wem	*from whom*
wessen	*whose*

Also useful are:

wohin	*where to*
wie oft	*how often*
welche	*which*
wie	*how*
wie lange	*how long*
was für	*what kind of*
wie viel	*how much*
wie viele	*how many*
bis wann	*until when*

1 Self, Family & Friends

1 **a** Onkel; **b** Haustier; **c** hässlich;
d Tante; **e** Sohn

2 der Großvater - die Großmutter;
der Bruder - die Schwester; der Onkel
- die Tante; der Sohn - die Tochter;
der Vetter - die Kusine

3 **a** Vater Mutter Sohn Vetter
Tochter Onkel Kusine Großvater

b Katze Wellensittich Vogel
Kaninchen Hamster Pferd Hund
Maus

4 **a** Haar; **b** Freund; **c** Geburtstag;
d Taschengeld; **e** Erwachsene

5 alt - jung; dick - schlank;
schwach – stark; schön - hässlich;
lang - kurz; hell - dunkel

6 **1** Oma; **2** Opa; **3** Onkel;
4 Mutter; **5** Tante; **6** Sohn;
7 Tochter

7 **Körper:** Bart, Glatze, Auge,
Haar, Nase

Haustier: Kaninchen, Hund,
Meerschweinchen, Ratte,
Wellensittich

Familie: Vetter, Geschwister,
Zwilling, Erwachsene, Großeltern

8 mittelgroß; buchstabieren; Geburt;
Stiefvater; verheiratet

2 Local Area & Weather

1 **a** sonnig; **b** schneien (es schneit);
c heiß; **d** wolkig *or* bewölkt;
e es regnet; **f** windig; **g** kalt

2 **a** der Bahnhof; **b** die Brücke;
c die Kirche; **d** das Krankenhaus;
e der Marktplatz;
f das Denkmal; **g** das Kino

3 **a** der Fluss; **b** die Kirche;
c die Kuh; **d** das Dorf;
e der Hügel; **f** die Sonne;
g das Schaf

4 **Stadt:** Dom; Fußgängerzone;
Wohngebiet; Krankenhaus; Theater

Land: Dorf; Hügel; Fluss; Schaf; Feld

Wetter: Schauer; schwül;
Gewitter; Donner; Blitz

5 Jugendklub; Sonnenaufgang;
Krankenhaus; Einkaufszentrum;
Wettervorhersage; Schwimmbad;
Höchsttemperatur; Bahnübergang

6 heiß - kalt; kühl - warm;
nass - trocken; bewölkt - wolkenlos;
Sonnenaufgang - Sonnenuntergang.

7 **a** die Fußgängerzone;
b der Bahnhof; **c** der Park;
d das Krankenhaus;
e das Freibad;
f das Theater; **g** der Jugendklub

8 **a** Fluss; **b** Einwohner;
c hitzefrei; **d** Feld; **e** Dorf;
f Kino; **g** Schnee; **h** Nähe

3 School Life

1 **Fächer:** Erdkunde, Geschichte, Kunst, Werken, Informatik, Turnen

Sachen: Buch, Heft, Bleistift, Ordner, Lineal

Zimmer: Labor, Turnhalle, Kantine, Klassenzimmer, Bibliothek

Personen: Schüler, Schuldirektor, Lehrer, Primaner

2 **a** Erdkunde; **b** Religion; **c** Informatik; **d** Geschichte; **e** Mathe *or* Mathematik; **f** Chemie; **g** Kunst; **h** Französisch

3 **a** Schüler; **b** Physik, Chemie, Biologie (*any order*); **c** Ferien; **d** Hausaufgaben; **e** Grundschule; **f** Kantine; **g** Französisch

4 **a** der Bleistift; **b** das Heft; **c** der Kugelschreiber (der Kuli); **d** das Wörterbuch; **e** das Buch; **f** das Lineal; **g** das Papier.

5 Informatik – der Computer; das Labor – Chemie; die Bibliothek – das Buch; Turnen – die Turnhalle; das Wörterbuch – Französisch; Mathematik – das Lineal; die Prüfung – pauken

6 **a** das Gymnasium; **b** der Stundenplan; **c** die Turnhalle; **d** das Zeugnis; **e** die Schulreise; **f** die Hausaufgaben

7 Kassettenrekorder; Kugelschreiber; Hauptschule; Stundenplan; Lieblingsfach; Wörterbuch; Schuldirektor; Mittagspause; Turnhalle; Hausaufgaben

4 The Future: Education & Work

Education

1 die Schule, die Oberstufe, das Abitur, bestehen, studieren, das Vorstellungsgespräch, der Beruf

2 die Mittlere Reife, das Abitur, die Qualifikation, durchfallen, bestehen, studieren, der Erfolg

3 Lebenslauf, Leistung, Lehre; Stellenanzeige, studieren, Student; Abitur, Arzt, Ausbildung; Beruf, berufstätig, Berufsausbildung

4 **a** Tierarzt; **b** Zukunft; **c** Lehrling; **d** Feierabend; **e** Ausbildung; **f** studieren

Work

1 **a** der Briefträger; **b** der Bäcker; **c** der Koch; **d** der Kassierer; **e** der Mechaniker; **f** der Zahnarzt; **g** die Sekretärin; **h** der Polizist

2 **a** der Journalist; **b** der Mechaniker; **c** die Luftstewardess; **d** der Krankenpfleger *or* die Krankenschwester; **e** der Briefträger; **f** der Kassierer; **g** die Hausfrau; **h** der Beamte

3 **a** der Kassierer; der Kaufmann *or* die Kauffrau; der Krankenpfleger *or* die Kranken-schwester **b** die Fabrik, die Firma, das Büro **c** der Bäcker, der Briefträger, der Buchhalter, der Beamte

4 Arbeitgeber, arbeitslos, Arbeitspraktikum, Briefträger, Hausfrau, Kaufmann, Krankenpfleger, Teilzeitjob

5 Travel & Transport

1 Busbahnhof; Autobahnnetz; Bushaltestelle; Rückfahrkarte; Windschutzscheibe; Luftkissenfahrzeug; Einzelfahrkarte

2 **Auto:** der Kofferraum; die Bundesstraße; die Ringstraße; der Stau; überholen

Zug: der Schlafwagen; der Kontrolleur; der Wartesaal; das Gleis; der Zuschlag

Flugzeug: der Flughafen; der Luftsteward; fliegen; landen; die Landung

3 **a** der Scheinwerfer; **b** das Auto *or* der Wagen; **c** der Bus; **d** der Reifen; **e** das Fahrrad; **f** das Flugzeug; **g** der Zug; **h** das Luftkissenfahrzeug

4 einsteigen; abfahren; fahren; überholen; ankommen; aussteigen; zurückkommen

5 **a** Sitzplatz; Parkplatz

b Fahrbahn; Autobahn; Eisenbahn

c Abfahrt; Ausfahrt; Heimfahrt

6 **a** Führerschein; **b** Fahrplan; **c** Rückfahrkarte; **d** Busbahnhof; **e** Stoßzeit; **f** Fahrrad, Zweirad; **g** Autobus; **h** Flughafen

7 **a** Verspätung; **b** Wartesaal; **c** Führerschein; **d** Kofferraum; **e** Parkplatz; **f** Stau; **g** Flughafen; **h** zu Fuß

8 Schalter, Scheinwerfer, Schlafwagen Gepäck, Gepäckablage, Gepäckaufbewahrungsstelle Fahrer, Fahrplan, Fahrkarte Auspuff, Ausweis, Ausfahrt

6 Holidays, Tourism & Tourist Information

1 **a** die Rundfahrt; **b** die Reise; **c** das Meer; **d** buchen; **e** das Touristenbüro; **f** der Urlaub

2 **Landschaft:** der Berg, der See, der Strand, die Insel, die Küste

Tour: besichtigen, die Pauschalreise, die Stadtrundfahrt, die Sehenswürdigkeit, der Turm

Person: der Reiseleiter, der Rettungsschwimmer der Urlauber, der Tourist

3 a Küste *or* See; b Blick; c Strand;
d sonnen uns; e Balkon;
f Ausflüge; g Reiseleiter;
h gebucht; i Broschüren

4 a 4; b 5; c 3; d 1; e 2

5 a der Berg *or* das Gebirge;
b der Balkon; c der Strand;
d die See *or* das Meer;
e die Sesselbahn *or* der Sessellift;
f der Picknickplatz; g das Boot;
h der Turm; i der Reiseleiter

7 Accommodation

1 a die Zahnbürste; b die Zahnpasta;
c die Dusche; d der Schlüssel;
e das Zelt; f der Schlafsack;
g die Seife

2 a H; b C; c B; d H; e H;
f B; g B; h C; i H; j B; k C

3 a der Aufzug; der Lift

b das Doppelzimmer;
das Einzelzimmer;
das Familienzimmer;
Fremdenzimmer

c der Empfang; die Rezeption

4 Rasierapparat   Waschbecken
Aufzug   Wohnwagen
Jugendherberge   Unterkunft
Vollpension   Zeltplatz

5 Schlafsack; Schlüssel; Seife
Rezeption; Reservierung;
Rasierapparat

6 a Wir übernachten in der
Jugendherberge./ Wir zelten auf dem
Campingplatz.

b Wir bekommen Halbpension:
Frühstück und Abendessen./Wir
bekommen Vollpension: Frühstück,
Mittagessen und Abendessen.

c Wir essen in dem Speisesaal im
Hotel.

d Mein Bruder und ich schlafen in
einem Doppelzimmer.

8 People & Places

1 a England; b Frankreich;
c Griechenland; d Amerika;
e Italien; f Belgien;
g Schottland; h Österreich;
i Spanien; j Deutschland

2 England - englisch - der Engländer
Deutschland - deutsch - der Deutsche
Frankreich - französisch - der
Franzose
Italien - italienisch - der Italiener
Griechenland - griechisch - der
Grieche
Spanien - spanisch - der Spanier
die Türkei - türkisch - der Türke
die Schweiz - schweizerisch - der
Schweizer

3 a Englisch; b Französisch;
c Deutsch; d Italienisch;
e Spanisch; f Griechisch;
g Türkisch; h Portugiesisch

4 a die Ostsee; b die Nordsee;
c Köln; d München; e Bayern;
f die Alpen; g der Rhein;
h Berlin

5 a die Ostsee; b die Nordsee;
   c der Kanal; d Wien;
   e das Mittelmeer; f die Schweiz;
   g die Alpen

6 a Großbritannien; b Frankreich;
   c Spanien; d Deutschland;
   e Österreich; f Belgien;
   g die Schweiz; h Italien

7 a Italien; b Frankreich;
   c England or Großbritannien;
   d Amerika; e Deutschland

8 a Brieffreund; b die Donau;
   c italienisch; d die Nordsee;
   e Bayern; f Franzose;
   g das Mittelmeer; h Europa

9 Services & Finding the Way

Services

1 Post, Postkarte, Postamt
  Telefonat, Telefonkarte, Telefonzelle /
  telefonieren
  Anruf, Ansichtskarte, anrufen

2 a die Briefmarke;
   b die Postkarte;
   c der Briefkasten;
   d die Vorwahlnummer;
   e das Kleingeld

3 a wechseln; b schicken;
   c mailen; d wählen

4 Making a telephone call.

  den Hörer abnehmen;
  Geld einwerfen; wählen;
  verbinden; sprechen;
  Auf Wiederhören sagen;
  den Hörer auflegen.

5 a Brief; b schicken;
   c Postkarte; d Telefonzelle;
   e Telefonkarte

Finding the Way

1 a geradeaus; b links; c rechts;
   d die Ampel; e die Kreuzung;
   f die Ecke; g der Wegweiser;
   h das Schild

2 hinter - vor; links - rechts;
  erste - letzte; suchen - finden

3 a Entschuldigung!; b suche;
   c Wo; d Stadtplan; e finden;
   f gehen; g geradeaus;
   h Nehmen; i erste; j links;
   k rechten; l ungefähr

4 a Kreuzung; b Stadtplan;
   c überqueren; d Einbahnstraße;
   e geradeaus; f Landkarte;
   g Wegweiser

10 Accidents, Injuries & Illness

1 a der Kopf; b das Gesicht;
   c der Hals; d die Schulter;
   e die Brust; f der Arm;
   g der Bauch; h die Hand;
   i der Finger; j das Bein;
   k das Knie; l der Fuß

2 **a** das Haar; **b** das Auge;
 c das Ohr; **d** die Nase;
 e der Zahn (die Zähne);
 f der Mund;
 g die Zunge

3 **a** V; **b** V; **c** K; **d** K; **e** G;
 f G; **g** K; **h** V; **i** G

4 **a** Fieber; **b** verboten;
 c Tablette; **d** gesund

5 **a** die Hand; **b** die Stimme;
 c der Fuß *or* das Bein; **d** das Ohr;
 e der Sonnenbrand;
 f die Magenschmerzen;
 g die Ohrenschmerzen

6 **a** Ich habe eine Erkältung.
 b Ich muss Tabletten nehmen.
 c Vorsicht!
 d Ich habe Fieber.
 e Mir ist übel.

7 **a** das Aspirin, die Hand, der Finger,
 der Arm

8 das Blut, der Mund, die Brust,
 die Lippe, die Medizin, die Pille,
 die Schulter, die Zunge,
 das Knie, das Ohr

11 House & Home

1 **a** das Bad **b** der Tisch
 c der Geschirrspülautomat; der
 Kühlschrank; die Waschmaschine;
 der Herd **d** das Auto
 e das Bett; der Kleiderschrank
 f der Sessel; der Fernseher

2 **a** die Lampe; **b** der Fernseher;
 c der Tisch; **d** der Stuhl;
 e der Spiegel; **f** der Teppich;
 g die Blume; **h** die Stereoanlage;
 i das Telefon; **j** die Tür

3 **a** der Wohnblock;
 b das Einfamilienhaus;
 c das Doppelhaus;
 d der Bungalow;
 e die Wohnung

4 **a** Doppelhaus, Einfamilienhaus,

 b Badezimmer, Esszimmer,
 Schlafzimmer, Wohnzimmer

 c Heizung, Wohnung, Zentralheizung

 d Keller, Mixer, CD-Spieler, Leiter,
 Wecker

5 **a** pocket; die Taschenlampe,
 torch

 b machine; die Waschmaschine,
 washing machine / die
 Spülmaschine, dishwasher

 c house; das Doppelhaus, semi-
 detached / das Einfamilienhaus,
 detached

 d room; das Badezimmer,
 bathroom / das Esszimmer, dining
 room / das Schlafzimmer, bedroom /
 das Wohnzimmer, living room

 e roof; der Dachboden, attic

6 **a** der Wecker; **b** der Spiegel;
 c die Treppe; **d** die Garage;
 e die Blume *or* die Pflanze;
 f der Keller; **g** die Möbel;
 h der Vorhang

7 **a** O; **b** U; **c** D; **d** O; **e** U;
f D; **g** B; **h** O; **i** B

8 das Dach; der Dachboden;
das Schlafzimmer; die Treppe;
der Kamin; der Keller

12 Life at Home

1 **a** aufwachen; **b** aufstehen;
c essen; **d** trinken;
e sich waschen; **f** duschen;
g schlafen; **h** kochen

2 e – d – h – a – g – b – c - f

3 **a** ich dusche mich; ich wasche
mich; ich putze mir die Zähne

b ich wache auf; ich stehe auf; ich
schlafe; der Wecker klingelt

c ich koche; ich esse; ich trinke

4 N, V, N, V, N, B, B, N

13 Special Occasions

1 **a** der Geburtstag; **b** Weihnachten;
c Ostern; **d** Neujahrstag;
e die Hochzeit; **f** die Verlobung;
g das Geschenk; **h** die Einladung

2 **a** Gute; **b** Weihnachten;
c gratuliere

3 e – c – g – b – a – f – d

4 **a** Weihnachten; **b** Pfingsten;
c Silvester; **d** Geburtstag

5 Neujahrstag - Ostern - Pfingsten -
Weihnachten - Silvester

14 Healthy Living

1 **a** F; **b** U; **c** F; **d** F; **e** F;
f F; **g** U; **h** U

2 **a** Athletik; **b** abnehmen;
c allergisch; **d** Werbung;
e Vegetarier; **f** Sportverein

3 **a** Rauchen; **b** Vegetarier;
c Sportverein; **d** abnehmen;
e mich entspannen;
f guter Gesundheit;
g im Bett

15 Food & Drink

1 **Gemüse:** Erbse, Blumenkohl,
Kartoffel, Kohl, Zwiebel

Getränke: Kaffee, Kakao,
Orangensaft, Wasser, Wein

Obst: Himbeere, Apfelsine, Pflaume,
Weintraube, Zitrone

2 **a** Apfel, Apfelsine, Pfirsich, Himbeere,
Banane, Zitrone, Erdbeere, Birne

b Bier, Wein, Kakao, Apfelsaft,
Tee, Cola, Wasser, Kaffee

3 Aprikose, Apfel, Apfelsine /
Apfelsaft
Brot, Brötchen, Bratwurst
Kalbfleisch, Kartoffel, Kakao
Schinken, Schokolade, Scheibe

4 die Kartoffel; der Schinken;
die Birne; der Reis; der Kohl;
der Pfeffer; das Salz; das Obst;
der Käse; die Wurst

5 **a** die Banane, die Zitrone

b die Bratwurst, die Currywurst, die Weißwurst, das Würstchen

c Erdbeere, Himbeere, Banane, Zitrone

d das Kalbfleisch, das Rindfleisch, das Schweinefleisch, der Schinken, der Speck

e die Butter, die Milch, der Käse, die Sahne

6 **a** Brot mit Butter;
b Fisch mit Pommes frites;
c Salz und Essig *or* Pfeffer;
d Erdbeeren mit Sahne;
e Milch und Zucker

7 **a** der Apfel; **b** die Erbse;
c die Zitrone; **d** die Zwiebel;
e der Schinken; **f** der Tee;
g die Chips

8 **a** der Apfel; **b** der Kaffee;
c der Käse; **d** das Bier;
e der Reis; **f** der Senf;
g der Tee; **h** die Kartoffel

16 Eating Out

1 **a** die Gabel; **b** der Löffel;
c das Messer; **d** das Glas;
e der Kellner; **f** der Topf;
g die Tasse; **h** die Untertasse

2 Schweinebraten - Fleisch, roast - meat;
Getränk - Bier, drink - beer;
Kännchen - Kaffee, pot - coffee;
Kellner - Trinkgeld, waiter - tip;

Nachspeise - Eis, pudding - ice-cream;
schmecken - lecker, to taste - tasty;
Vorspeise - Suppe, starter - soup

3 f, g, c, i, h, b, a, d, e

4 bestellen *or* Bedienung, bezahlen, Becher

Schale, schmecken, Schnitzel

Messer, Menü, Mehrwertsteuer

Tasse *or* Tisch, Topf, Teller

5 Speisekarte, bestellen, Vorspeise, Hauptgericht, Nachspeise, bezahlen, Trinkgeld

6 **a** das Restaurant, das Café, die Imbisshalle

b der Becher, die Tasse, das Glas

c die Vorspeise, das Hauptgericht, die Nachspeise

7 **a** Speisekarte; **b** probieren;
c Getränk; **d** Vorspeise;
e Wirtshaus

17 Leisure Activities

1 **a** reiten; **b** fernsehen; **c** segeln;
d singen; **e** lesen; **f** angeln;
g tanzen; **h** Rad fahren;
i fotografieren; **j** skateboarden

2 schwimmen - das Hallenbad;
musizieren - das Klavier;
lesen - die Lektüre;
treffen - ausgehen;
die Spieler - die Mannschaft

3 **a** der Roman, die Zeitung

b Schach, Tischtennis,

c der Sänger, die Geige,
das Klavier, das Schlagzeug,
das Lied

d der Eintrittspresis, der Film,
der Schauspieler, der Sitz,
die Vorstellung,

4 Angeln: A;   Badminton: P;
Fußball: M;   Rad fahren: A;
Reiten: A;   Rollschuh laufen: A;
Schach: P;   Schwimmen: A;
Tanzen: P;   Tennis: P;

5 **a** Theaterstück - play;
b Tischtennis - tabletennis;
c Fußball/Basketball -
football/basketball;
d Seifenoper - soap opera;
e Satellitenschüssel - satellite dish;
f Schauspieler - actor;
g Hallenbad/Freibad - indoor/open-
air swimming pool;
h Nachtklub - nightclub.

6 **a** singe; **b** sehe;
c schwimme; **d** fotografiere;
e sammle

7 geschwommen; besucht; geschossen;
getroffen; gelesen

a Ich habe meine Oma besucht.

b Ich bin im Hallenbad
geschwommen.

c Ich habe die Zeitung gelesen.

d Ich habe meine Freunde getroffen.

e Vor dem Konzert hat das
Orchester viel geübt.

8 **Lesen:** die Lektüre, der Krimi,
der Roman, die Wochenzeitung

Musik: das Klavier, die Geige,
das Lied, der Sänger, der Walkman

Kino: der Eintrittspreis, der
Gruselfilm, der Schauspieler,
die Vorstellung

18   People & Personalities

1 **a** arm; **b** faul; **c** freundlich;
d höflich; **e** schüchtern;
f traurig; **g** glücklich; **h** böse

2 **a** doof: - ; **b** launisch: - ;
c nett: + ; **d** unhöflich: - ;
e faul: - ; **f** ungeduldig: - ;
g freundlich: + ; **h** brav: +

3 **a** schüchtern, zufrieden, allein

b glücklich, freundlich, höflich,
ehrlich

c lockig, geschwätzig, fleißig, ruhig,
ungeduldig, selbstsüchtig,
gesprächig, witzig, vorsichtig

4 dumm - intelligent;   laut - leise;
glücklich: traurig;   faul - fleißig;
höflich - unhöflich;
reich - arm;   geduldig - ungeduldig;
geschwätzig - schüchtern

5 You can check your answers in the
list on pages 68-69.

6 **a** böse; **b** faul; **c** schüchtern;
d arm; **e** berühmter; **f** ernst;
g geschwätzig *or* gesprächig;
h ehrlich

19 Meeting people

1 letzte Woche; vorgestern; gestern; heute; morgen; übermorgen; nächste Woche; nächstes Jahr

2 a Samstag, der elfte Januar
  b Mittwoch, der zweiundzwanzigste März
  c Donnerstag, der neunzehnte Mai
  d Sonntag, der achte Dezember
  e Freitag, der dreißigste November
  f Dienstag, der fünfzehnte Oktober
  g Montag, der vierzehnte Juli
  h Donnerstag, der zwölfte August

3 a eine Minute; b ein Jahr;
  c eine Woche; d ein Tag;
  e das Wochenende; f ein Monat

4 a A; b L; c A; d L; e A;
  f L; g A; h A

5 a Samstag, Sonnabend
  b der Morgen, der Vormittag
  c sechs Uhr dreißig, halb sieben
  d jetzt, nun
  e jeden Tag, täglich

6 a Donnerstag; b Mittwoch;
  c Sonntag; d Freitag

7 a manchmal; b hoffentlich;
  c Termin; d Nachmittag;
  e Sonnabend

8 a Abend, Sonnabend: evening, Saturday;
  b kommen, willkommen: to come, welcome;
  c Mittag, Vormittag / Nachmittag: midday, morning / afternoon;
  d morgen, übermorgen: tomorrow, day after tomorrow;
  e gestern, vorgestern: yesterday, day before yesterday;
  f Woche, Wochenende: week, weekend;

9 a übermorgen (über 'mor' 'gen')
  b der Nachmittag ('der' nach 'Mittag')
  c ein langes Wochenende

20 Shopping & Money

1 a das Bonbon; b die Rolltreppe;
  c die Einkäufe; d die Dose;
  e die Kreditkarte;
  f der Zeitungskiosk; g die Kasse;
  h das Portemonnaie

2 a W; b M; c C; d C;
  e C + W; f C; g W

3 a die Bäckerei;
  b das Schreibwarengeschäft;
  c die Buchhandlung;
  d die Konditorei;
  e die Metzgerei;
  f das Lebensmittelgeschäft;
  g die Apotheke / die Drogerie

4 a offen;
  b Sonderangebote;
  c Auswahl; d Flasche; e Dose;
  f Dutzend; g Regal; h abteilung;
  i Kilo; j Kasse; k Quittung;
  l preiswert; m Tasche

5 **a** Tasche, Brieftasche: bag, wallet;
b Markt, Supermarkt: market, supermarket;
c Karte, Kreditkarte: ticket / map, credit card;
d Liste, Einkaufsliste: list, shopping list;
e kaufen, verkaufen: to buy, to sell;
f Fenster, Schaufenster: window, display window;
g Zeit / Öffnungszeiten: time, opening hours;
h Haus, Kaufhaus: house, department store;
i Geld, Bargeld: money, cash;
j geben, ausgeben: to give, to spend

6 ausverkauft, Buchhandlung, Lebensmittelgeschäft, Abteilung, Metzgerei, Einkaufsliste, Schaufenster, Untergeschoss, kostenlos

7 **a** die Bäckerei, die Buchhandlung, die Metzgerei, das Lebensmittelgeschäft, die Eisenwarenhandlung, das Warenhaus
b das Bargeld, der Scheck, die Kreditkarte
c die Dose, die Flasche, das Päckchen, das Paket
d das Gramm, das Kilo, das Pfund

21 Fashion & Clothes

1 **a** der Hut; **b** der Regenschirm;
c der Schuh; **d** die Hose;
e das Kleid; **f** die Krawatte / der Schlips; **g** das T-Shirt; **h** der Schal

2 **a** Arm, Armbandhur: arm, wristwatch
b Mantel, Regenmantel: overcoat, raincoat
c Wolle, Baumwolle: wool, cotton
d Lippen, Lippenstift: lips, lipstick
e Hose, Badehose: trousers, swimming trunks
f Schuh, Handschuh: shoe, glove
g Ring, Ohrringe: ring, earrings

3 **a** der Schlips, die Krawatte
b grau, grün, gelb
c der Pullover, der Ring, die Shorts, die Jeans
d anziehen, ausziehen, sich umziehen, vorziehen

4 **a** der Handschuh; **b** der Hut;
c die Ohrringe; **d** der Schal;
e die Socke / der Schuh;
f die Hose

5 **a** anprobieren; **b** Größe;
c Badehose; **d** Regenmantel, Regenschirm; **e** eingelaufen;
f bequem; **g** Reißverschluss

6 Kleidung, Krawatte, Kleid
Schal, Schlips, Schuh
Größe, grün / grau, Gürtel
Paar, Pullover, Parfüm

7 **a** grün; **b** gelb; **c** grau;
d rot, gelb (orange), grün; **e** rot;
f gelb, weiß; **g** rot, weiß, blau;
h rosa;
i rot, weiß, rot; **j** weiß

22 Current Affairs & Social Issues

1 **a** der Vandalismus;
b Ladendiebstahl; **c** der Alkohol;
d der Müll;
e die Wiederverwertung;
f die Umweltverschmutzung;
g die Obdachlosigkeit;
h die Arbeitslosigkeit; **i** der Lärm

2 **a** Laden, Ladendiebstahl: shop,
shoplifting

b Haus, Haushaltsmüll: house,
household refuse

c Umwelt, Umweltverschmutzung /
umweltfreundlich: environment,
pollution / environmentally friendly

d Ozon, Ozonschicht: ozone, ozone
layer

e wieder, Wiederverwertung: again,
recycling

f geben, ausgeben: to give, to spend

3 **a** schmutzig; **b** sparen;
c Einwanderer; **d** Rauchen;
e obdachlos; **f** Mehrwegflaschen

4 sauber = clean;   Dieb = thief;
Ebbe = low tide;   Welt = world;
Luft = air;   Regenwald = rainforest
Gewalt = violence;   Lärm = noise

Prepositions

1 **a** der **b** dem **c** einem
d meiner **e** meiner **f** dem
g zur (*zu der* is usually shortened to
zur) **h** meiner **i** dem **j** zum (*zu
dem* is usually shortened to *zum*)

2 **a** meine **b** die **c** meine
d den **e** deinen **f** den
g meinen **h** einen **i** den **j** das

3 **a** dem (or *meinem*) **b** dem
c der **d** der **e** dem **f** den
g der **h** ins (*in das* is usually
shortened to *ins*) **i** mein
j dem (or *meinem*)

4 **a** meiner **b** der **c** der
d meinem **e** dem **f** die
g der **h** dem, zur
i meinem, das (ins)
j dem, das (ins)